T0119125

The Financial History
of Cambridge University

The Financial History
of Cambridge University

Robert Neild

THAMES RIVER PRESS

The Financial History of Cambridge University

THAMES RIVER PRESS
An imprint of Wimbledon Publishing Company Limited (WPC)
Another imprint of WPC is Anthem Press (www.anthempress.com)

First published in the United Kingdom in 2012 by

THAMES RIVER PRESS
75-76 Blackfriars Road
London SE1 8HA

www.thamesriverpress.com

© Robert Neild 2012

All rights reserved. No part of this publication may be reproduced
in any form or by any means without written permission of the publisher.

The moral rights of the author have been asserted in accordance
with the Copyright, Designs and Patents Act 1988.

A CIP record for this book is available from the British Library.

ISBN 978-0-85728-515-7

The cover image is an illustration by John Tenniel from chapter 3,
'The Caucus-Race and a Long Tale', of Lewis Carroll's
Alice's Adventures in Wonderland (1865/6).

CONTENTS

ACKNOWLEDGEMENTS

I am indebted to many people in the university offices, the colleges and in other places who helped me in my pursuit of evidence.

Foremost are Paul Light, head of financial reporting in the university who has been extraordinarily patient and efficient in answering the many queries I have put to him about the university's complex modern accounts; and Jacqueline Cox, the university archivist, who, though grievously under-staffed, swiftly guided me to all kinds of documents relating to the early years. Others in the university offices to whom I am indebted are Andrew Reid, the director of finance, who spared me time to explain the university's investment policy; Lindsay Dane and Godfrey McMillan who provided me much information about the university's past land transactions; Graham Gale of the Development Office for statistics of fund-raising; Virginia Mitchell and Mike Sinclair for information on trusts; Wendy Solomou for information on student numbers; Dr Jeff Jones, the manager of the university farm for explaining to me its history and current operation; and Mr Noblett and his staff in the Official Publications Room of the University Library, surely the best library in the world.

At Trinity the library staff have been have been, as always, wonderfully kind and helpful. In particular, Jonathan Smith, the chief archivist, has traced material for me from many sources, and Andrew Lambert and his colleagues have saved my limbs by kindly climbing ladders and fetching books for me from the underground bookstore. Equally kind have been Hansa Chauhan and Elspeth Lindsey, the fellows secretaries, who helped me when my efforts to be my own secretary failed. Three postgraduate students – Elodie Partridge, Rebecca Whyte and Piing Chen – did various jobs for me extracting data and preparing statistical tables and charts.

I am indebted to a number of archivists at other colleges: Malcolm Underwood at St John's, Patricia McGuire at King's, Mrs Myers at Corpus, Kate Thompson at Downing and Dr Pollard at Trinity Hall.

Outside Cambridge I was helped by Mark Jones of the Higher Education Statistics Agency (HESA), by Nicola Hicks at the Higher Education Funding

Council (HEFCE), Hersh Mann of the UK Data Archive at the University of Essex; and by Don Powell of the Sanger Institute.

Gillian Sutherland, the late Tony Weir and David McKitterick were kind enough to read the book in draft and offer comments.

Tej Sood and Rob Reddick of Thames River Press have produced this book with wonderful efficiency in six months.

I am most grateful to them all.

PREFACE

I embarked on this book in order to get a long view of why Cambridge, which is repeatedly rated one of the world's best universities, has been cutting expenditure, appealing for money and, at the same time, losing its academic independence. My motive was curiosity. Retired for many years and free of claims on my time, I enjoy finding a question about the world around me (which has narrowed) and spending my days chasing statistics and other information that may help answer it. I last addressed the question, how did Trinity become so rich? To answer it, I delved into college accounts and other records that go back to 1547.[1]

Since the university, as distinct from the colleges, had little money till the late nineteenth century, this history starts only in 1850. That does not mean that there is little to record, for there have been huge changes in the character of the university since 1850, notably in the scale of scientific research, in the sources and scale of the university's income, in the social origin of students and in the relationship of the government to the university. I have used the financial records and other statistics to show the nature and scale of those changes. To interpret them and bring them to life I have described as briefly and lightly as possible the surrounding economic and social tides, and the persons, some comic, many larger than life, who have populated this little universe and helped to change it.

I hope that my findings will interest, and sometimes amuse, those who are curious about the university's history, and that they may be helpful to those who debate and shape its present policies. I have not attempted to recommend what those policies should now be. I have spent enough of my life doing that.

Robert Neild
Trinity College
Cambridge
February 2012

---

1 Robert Neild, *Riches and Responsibility: the Financial History of Trinity College, Cambridge* (2008).

LIST OF TABLES AND CHARTS

Tables

Charts

Chapter 1

FINANCIAL INFANCY AND REFORM

In the middle of the nineteenth century the University of Cambridge, as distinct from the colleges, scarcely existed as a financial entity. Most of the money and nearly all the grand buildings of Cambridge belonged to the colleges, which, with one recently created exception, Downing College, were ecclesiastical establishments whose traditional function was to produce educated clergy.[1]

The heads of the colleges, known as the 'heads of house', were the rulers of the university and enjoyed great privileges. Unlike college fellows, they were permitted to marry and were provided with a master's lodge where they might live with their families within the college. Oligarchs, they dominated their colleges and took it in turn to serve a year at a time as vice-chancellor of the university, which, governed by Elizabethan statutes, performed such functions as organising exams, granting degrees, appointing professors, performing ceremonial functions, providing a library, settling disciplinary cases and disputes through its own courts, and supervising the town's markets. Its only buildings were the Old Schools, the Senate House, the Observatory and the Fitzwilliam Museum. The chancellor was a grandee from the outer world who was expected to represent the university beyond its bounds, not trespass on the territory of the heads of house.

The royal commission of 1922 described the position in 1852 succinctly:

> The colleges were still everything, the University nothing save an abstraction, or at most, an examining body.[2]

These words were probably written by G. M. Trevelyan, a member of the commission who is reported to have been mainly responsible for the descriptions of Cambridge in the commission's report.[3]

---

1 The statutes of Downing, which received its royal charter in 1800, required it to have only two fellows in holy orders. See Stanley French, *The History of Downing College Cambridge* (1978), 82.

2 *Report of the Royal Commission on Oxford and Cambridge Universities* (1922), 20.

3 Christopher N. L. Brooke, *A History of the University of Cambridge, 1870–1990* (1993), 368.

The colleges had been financially dominant from the beginning since benefactors, whether monarchs or subjects, liked to imprint a name and impose their ideas on a college, something they could not do to the university.[4] The university's few benefactions were mostly for professorships. The endowments of both the colleges and university consisted almost entirely of land, which until modern times was the only safe income-earning asset an individual or institution could hold.[5]

The Poverty of the University

The royal commission of 1852 estimated the endowment income of the colleges, including trusts earmarked for named purposes, at not less than £185,000, rents having been swelled in the eighteenth century by agricultural improvement.[6] The university's endowment income came to only one twentieth of that figure – £9,000, most of which was in trusts. Only £3,000 – the greater part of which came from a single property at Burwell near Cambridge – was free to be used as the university chose. Fees for matriculation and degrees, together with compulsory library contributions, brought in £6,000, and Parliament annually voted £1,000 a year in support of some named professorships (Table 1.1).

At this time Britain was displaying its industrial achievements at the Great Exhibition, but Cambridge, like Oxford, was a quasi-monastic backwater: Catholics, Jews and non-conformists were effectively deterred from entry by the rule that to get a degree they had to subscribe to the 39 Articles of Anglican

Table 1.1. The composition of the university's income, 1845–51 average

	£
Endowment income: free	3,000
Endowment income: in trust	6,000
Fees and dues	6,000
Government	1,000
Other	1,000
Total	17,000

Source: *Report of the Cambridge University Commission* (1852), 'Evidence from the University', 15–16.

---

4 *Report of the Royal Commission on Oxford and Cambridge Universities* (1922), 13.

5 In 1871 the colleges of Cambridge owned 124,826 acres of landed estates, the university 2,445 acres. *Report of the Royal Commission on Oxford and Cambridge* (1874), I: 26.

6 *Report of the Cambridge University Commission* (1852), 197.

church and thereby renounce their faith; women were not admitted; fellows had to be celibate and mostly in holy orders. The heads of house resisted change that would diminish their power. Understandably, the regime was increasingly criticised from inside and out, in particular for the lack of provision for the study of natural sciences. Financial reform was not initially uppermost, but it was recognised that the university badly needed money in order to employ more professors and lecturers, and to create central museums, laboratories and other facilities for new subjects, mostly in the natural sciences. There was also an urgent need to reform the pay of existing professors, some of whom received little because the property with which their professorship was endowed was poor, while others received much from rich endowments. The differences were enormous. The richest was the Lady Margaret Professorship of Divinity which in 1852 enjoyed rent of over £1,800 from a property given by James I in 1605. Others got £100 or less. In 1882, after reform, the pay of nearly all the professors was in the range £700 to £850 (Table 1.2). Tortuous procedures were sometimes necessary to achieve that realignment. An example, described in Appendix 1A, is the remuneration of the three regius professorships that were attached to Trinity at its foundation.

One can see four sources from which the university might have sought money, and the obstacles to each:

1. Appeals for money: In the eighteenth century, the university had raised money by appeals to pay for building the Senate House and, later, for the classical facade of the Old Schools that stands at right angles to the Senate House. Together the two appeals slowly brought in £21,000, of which no less than £8,000, was contributed by the monarch: £2,000 by George I and £6,000 by George II.[7] After the Napoleonic Wars, appeals did less well. In the 1830s the university adopted a plan to build a grand quadrangle to take the place of the Old Schools and the old buildings to its west, which the university had just bought from King's College and which are now part of the Old Schools complex. Both sets of buildings were to be demolished. The new quadrangle was to house museums and schools for new subjects, surmounted by a new library on the whole of the first floor. With insufficient money in prospect, the plan was dropped.[8] Instead, an appeal was launched for the building of only a new library on the north side of the site. £23,000 (in money eroded by wartime inflation) was raised

---

7 J. W. Clark, *Endowments of the University of Cambridge* (1904), 453–67.

8 Robert Willis and John Willis Clark, *The Architectural History of the University of Cambridge* (1886), III: 114–21; and David Watkin, *The Life and Work of C. R. Cockerell* (1974), 183–7.

but the cost of the building was £35,000.[9] The largest contributions listed are £500 each from the chancellor (Lord Camden), the high steward (the Duke of Northumberland) and the Bishop of Ely. A little earlier Trinity had appealed for money to pay for the building of its New Court and had been left with large debts; the poor response was attributed to the impact on landowners of the fall in food prices that followed the end of the Napoleonic Wars.[10] Three other colleges that constructed major new buildings at this time of rising student numbers did not make appeals. Corpus and King's had each accumulated over many decades a building fund sufficient to meet all, or most of, the cost of their new buildings. St John's, having accumulated a little, borrowed a lot and landed in financial difficulties.[11]

2. The colleges: Some were rich but, predictably, there was opposition to the surrender of college income to the university.

3. The government: It had committed itself, mostly in the eighteenth century, to financing a few professorships. By the 1850s however the government was no more likely to offer money to the heads of house that ran the university than the latter were likely to ask the government for money, knowing that the price they would have to pay would be reform entailing the surrender of their oligarchic power. There was one exception: in 1858 the government at the request of the university repealed stamp duties on matriculation and degrees, which had been costing the university £3,000 a year. In return the university took over payments for professorships that had been costing the government £1,000 a year, leaving a net gain to the university of £2,000.[12]

4. Fees charged to students: The university charged fees of three kinds: matriculation fees (meaning fees for admission to the university), fees for degrees (awarded at the end of the typical student's time in residence), and a capitation tax, first introduced in 1825 to help finance the library. The last was levied on 'members of the university', meaning not only resident

---

9 Known as the Cockerell Building after its architect, it was occupied by the university library till 1934 when it was moved to its present building, and then by the law and history libraries till they were moved on to new buildings on Sidwick Avenue later in the twentieth-century. The building was then sold on a 999-year lease to Gonville and Caius College for use as its college library.

10 In gratitude to George IV who gave £1,000 to the appeal, the court was at first called King's Court.

11 Willis and Clark, *The Architectural History of the University of Cambridge*, I: 298–302, and 536–65 and H. F Howard, *An Account of the Finances of the College of St John the Evangelist* (1935), 165–9.

12 21 Vic. Cap. XI, 1858, reproduced in: *Statutes of the University of Cambridge with some Acts of Parliament Relating to the University* (1882), 154–5. The proposal is to be found in *Report of the Cambridge University Commission* (1852), 'Evidence from the University', 140.

students but also past students who, if they paid this modest charge, retained their link with the university and had a vote as members of the Senate, the ultimate ruling body of the university. All these fees were collected by the colleges and paid into the university chest (the central kitty), an arrangement that combined simplicity of collection with a pooling of funds appropriate to an era when costs of teaching did not vary much from subject to subject.

The matriculation fees were differentiated according to the rank of the entrant, which must have been roughly related to his ability to pay (Table 2.1). A nobleman (whose privileges included being awarded a degree without taking an exam, eating with the fellows on the High Table of his college and not having to observe residence requirements) was made to pay about three times as much as a pensioner (meaning one of the fee-paying students) who by this time made up the bulk of the student body; a fellow commoner, who enjoyed much the same privileges as a nobleman, paid twice as much as a pensioner. At the other extreme less than £1 was demanded of sizars, the term for those undergraduates who, in the days before entrance scholarships, were admitted on the recommendation of their schoolmaster and had the opportunity to compete for a scholarship once in residence. They were obliged to wait on High Table and were fed on the High Table food that was left over after Hall, rather than on the common meal given to undergraduates. Isaac Newton and many other distinguished men were admitted this way.

Table 1.2. Fees charged for matriculation, 1825 and 1842

	£. s.d.	
	1825	1842
Nobleman	£5	£16
Fellow Commoner	£3	£11
Pensioner	£1 10 0	£5 10 0
Sizar	£0 15 0	£0 15 0

The royal commission of 1852 reported that 'Great expense having been incurred by the University in the purchase of site and the erection of buildings for various academical purposes... it became necessary to raise the charges on students at Matriculation and Degrees on several occasions' and gave figures showing that between 1825 and 1842 the matriculation fee had been increased threefold or more for all but sizars.[13] In 1848 a proposal for a further increase had been rejected.

---

13 *Report of the Cambridge University Commission* (1852), 139.

Such was the situation when battle was joined over reform in the mid 1850s. After a thirty-year war, on which more later, the outcome as regards finance was this:

1. The university had assumed responsibility for the pay of professors and had nearly standardised their pay through a variety of measures: topping up inadequate benefactions; taking over other benefactions; and giving new professorships similar pay to one another. A list of professors and of their pay before and after reform is shown in Appendix 1B, at the end of the chapter.
2. The colleges had all been made to pay a fraction of their income to the university under a scheme known as the university contribution, to be spent on a list of specified purposes, the first of which was the pay of more professors, readers and university lecturers.[14]
3. The number of professorships had been increased from 25 to 36 and a considerable number of lectureships and readerships had been created.
4. To permit most university professors to enjoy the benefits of a college fellowship in addition to their university pay, each college had accepted an obligation to appoint one or more professorial fellows, the number determined by the wealth of the college, or suffer a financial penalty in the calculation of how much they had to pay towards the university contribution.[15]

There were two main rounds in the struggle for reform that brought about these changes. In each the government appointed a royal commission to report on the wealth of the university and colleges of Oxford and Cambridge, and subsequently appointed a statutory commission for each university to oversee reform, giving it little power or guidance at the first round, much at the second. There was a stark political problem to be faced: only the state could change the detailed statutes that had been imposed on Oxford and Cambridge in Tudor and Stuart times, yet at these, the only universities in England till the nineteenth century, there was powerful opposition to any state interference.

The First Royal Commission[16]

The first royal commission was appointed by Lord John Russell in 1850. In 1848 he had received a petition by 133 Cambridge graduates, 62 Oxford

---

14 *Statutes of the University of Cambridge* (1882), B, I.
15 *Statutes of the University of Cambridge* (1882), B, III.
16 In the following paragraphs I have been guided by: D. A. Winstanley, *Later Victorian Cambridge* (1947) and Elisabeth Leedham-Green, *A Concise History of the University of Cambridge* (1996). I have drawn on, and in places reproduced verbatim, passages from my recent book: Robert Neild, *Riches and Responsibility: the Financial History of Trinity College, Cambridge* (2008).

graduates and 29 Fellows of the Royal Society, calling for a royal commission to enquire into the best ways of reforming Oxford and Cambridge. Among the Cambridge signatories were Charles and Erasmus Darwin, Charles Babbage, Thackeray and Kinglake.[17] In response to strong agitation for and against reform, Russell appointed separate royal commissions for Oxford and Cambridge, each instructed to 'enquire into the state, discipline, studies and revenues' of the university and colleges. But the known resistance of the heads of house to the very notion of an enquiry into their affairs was so strong that the government trod cautiously and gave no power to compel information. At Oxford, the royal commission was completely cold-shouldered by the colleges and no information was provided. At Cambridge 5 of the 17 colleges – Caius, Clare, Corpus, Jesus and St Catharine's – refused to supply information about their finances.

After the university had failed adequately to heed the cautious suggestions of the royal commission, a Cambridge University Act was passed in 1856 which (a) replaced oligarchic rule of the university with representative government through a council elected by senior members of the university resident in Cambridge; and (b) created a statutory commission of eight Cambridge men, including some who had risen to distinction in the law and church, to whom it gave the task of trying, by negotiation, to induce the colleges and the university to change their ways. After five years, the outcome was a university that had a workable constitution written in English, not Latin; that was less permissive, was shorn of a clutch of eighteenth-century sinecures; and within which some of the colleges had adopted less oligarchic statutes. But no change was made in the financial balance between the colleges and the university: only three colleges agreed to the proposal that all the colleges should contribute a fraction of their income to the university.[18] The colleges sought to defy the university, rather as American states have defended their rights against the federal government in Washington as regards to tax and other matters. The commissioners in their final report in 1861 were, by their standards, outspoken:

...it was obvious that there would be required a large addition to the resources of the University at present available for the payment of Professors and Lecturers, and this addition the Royal Commissioners recommended should be supplied by a contribution to be made by the several Colleges. It is to the failure of our attempts to derive assistance from this source that we must mainly ascribe the imperfect manner in which we have been able to remedy the existing defects in the Professorial arrangements of the University.[19]

17 Peter Searby, *A History of the University of Cambridge, Vol. III, 1750–1870* (1997), 518–23.
18 Searby, *A History of the University of Cambridge*, 534–6.
19 *Report of the Cambridge University Commissioners* (1861), 5.

The Second Royal Commission

Ten years later Gladstone's Universities Tests Act cleared away religious discrimination 'with the happy effect of extricating future controversy about Oxford and Cambridge from the atmosphere of party politics in which till then it had to some extent moved.'[20] In the following year, 1872, Gladstone appointed the second royal commission to 'inquire into the property and income' of Oxford and Cambridge and also to 'report the uses to which such property and income are applied, together with all matters of fact tending to exhibit the state and circumstances of the same'.[21] The commission was not to make recommendations, but this was a wide remit to lay bare the facts for the benefit of those in the government and around it that shaped government policy. The two vice-chancellors promised that their respective universities and colleges would render the commission every facility, and they did so with the exception of Sidney Sussex, Cambridge, where Robert Phelps, the master, refused to provide the figures asked for, and prevented the fellows doing so by appointing himself bursar and removing the books to his lodge, from which he wrote insolent replies to the commission's requests for information.[22]

In 1874, after Disraeli had replaced Gladstone as prime minister, the commission delivered its report: fourteen pages of dry facts backed by hundreds of pages of financial statistics and explanatory material submitted by the two universities and their colleges. In the words of Winstanley, the facts revealed that 'the incomes of many colleges, in striking contrast to the incomes of the Universities, were greatly in excess of what they required for educational purposes'.[23] A year earlier a royal commission on scientific instruction and the advancement of science had called for the creation of science scholarships at Oxford and Cambridge (comparable to those for classics), for the end of celibacy, and the reform of the conditions of employment of professors and other teachers. The commission, which was chaired by the seventh Duke of Devonshire (on whom more in the next chapter), had gathered evidence on the superiority of scientific education in Germany and had been sent a petition calling for reform signed by 142 Cambridge dons, including 26 of the 33 professors, and 66 of the 84 lecturers and assistant tutors.[24]

---

20 *Report of the Royal Commission* (1922), 21.
21 Oxford and Cambridge had been opened to non-Anglicans by Gladstone's Universities Tests Act of 1871.
22 See *Report of the Royal Commission on Oxford and Cambridge* (1874), I: 24; III: 500–501.
23 Winstanley, *Later Victorian Cambridge*, 265.
24 *Third Report of the Royal Commission on Scientific Instruction and the Advancement of Science* (1873), appendix IV, lxiv–lxv. The deficiency of scientific education in Britain was repeatedly pointed out at this time. For example, 'In the matter of education we seem

Faced by the reports of these two royal commissions and by the growing tide of pressure for university reform, Disraeli on coming to power committed himself to the cause. Lord Salisbury tested the water in 1876 by introducing a Bill in the House of Lords for the reform of Oxford. After his Bill had received a favourable reception it was withdrawn, and the government in February 1877 introduced into the Commons a Bill for the reform of both universities that had teeth.

The Act of 1877

The resulting Act which came into force on 10 August 1877 appointed a statutory commission for each university, gave it power to impose new statutes on that university and on all of its colleges, and stated in detail what the object of those statutes should be.[25] For the universities, seventeen objects were listed, starting with:

> For enabling or requiring the several Colleges, or any of them, to make contribution out of their revenues for University purposes, regard being first had to the wants of the several Colleges in themselves for educational and other collegiate purposes.

The university and colleges were given the power to prepare new statutes along the prescribed lines and submit them for the approval of the commissioners before the end of 1878, after which the commissioners were empowered to impose new statutes on them. Many of the prescribed reforms had to do with such matters as the number of clerical fellowships, tenure, scholarships and teaching, but perhaps because the case for reform was now widely accepted, these did not arouse such prolonged controversy as the university contribution. Nor did two improvements in financial management, namely, the introduction of standard accounts at all colleges and the university, and the creation of a financial board of eleven members (of whom four were to be elected by the colleges with the votes weighted according to the income of the college) to manage the university's property

---

to be particularly deficient as compared with our foreign competitors; and this remark applies not only to what is usually called technical education, but to the ordinary commercial education which is required in mercantile house, and especially the knowledge of foreign languages.' *Final Report of the Royal Commission on the Depression in Trade and Industry* (1886), 97. Chaired by Stafford Northcote, first Earl of Iddesleigh, best known for the Northcote–Trevelyan report on civil service reform.

25 See the Universities of Oxford and Cambridge Act 1877 (40 and 41 Vict. c. 48), 16.

and income, a task hither performed by the vice-chancellor with limited assistance.[26]

By now few disputed that the colleges should make a financial contribution to the university, but many disputed the scale and details of the scheme proposed by the commissioners. On 15 December 1879, the *Cambridge University Reporter* published a hostile memorial from 197 fellows calling for an easing of the proposals, in particular for a statutory ceiling on how high the contribution could be raised in the future. Two days later there followed in the *Reporter* a memorial from just over 100 fellows supporting the proposals but suggesting amendments. Further, in 1880 the provost and fellows of King's College took up much the same case as had been made by the 197 fellows and appealed to the Universities Committee of the Privy Council, a body specially established to hear petitions against the statutes proposed by the commissioners.[27] The college's petition, elegantly argued by lawyers and printed, was met by a response in similar form by the commissioners.[28] But nothing more seems to have happened. No mention of the petition is to be found in the records of the Universities Committee of the Privy Council, and no ceiling was introduced into the formula.[29] Probably King's withdrew, but no record of a decision to withdraw could be found in the college's archives.

The statutory commissioners, amongst whom were the Lord Chief Justice, the Bishop of Worcester and Lord Rayleigh, did not flinch. They insisted that the statutes of every college should contain a provision that 'the college shall pay annually to the University the sum authorised by the statutes of the University'; and they adopted the formula that the total contribution by the colleges should start at £5,000 to £6,000 for the year 1884 and should rise in steps every three years to £30,000, and that each college should pay the same percentage of its income, with that percentage being calculated to produce the required total contribution, subject to a proviso that if the income of the colleges fell so low that the charge would be an excessive burden on them, the charge might be diminished.[30] A new standard system of college accounts was designed to produce a common basis for the assessment of the contribution.

---

26 Winstanley, *Later Victorian Cambridge*, 315–16; and *Statutes of the University of Cambridge* (1882), B, IV.

27 See the Universities of Oxford and Cambridge Act 1877 (40 and 41 Vict. c. 48), 44–8.

28 King's College Cambridge Archives, KCS/1.

29 I am grateful to the staff at the National Archives for searching the files. A petition by an individual fellow of King's concerning a statute that affected his personal position was found, not the petition by the provost and fellows.

30 Winstanley, *Later Victorian Cambridge*, 355; and *Statutes of the University of Cambridge* (1882), B, I.

Two factors intensified resistance to the university contribution: the agricultural depression and the dividend system.

The agricultural depression started in the early 1870s when food prices were driven down as cheap produce flooded into Britain's unprotected markets from the Americas and the antipodes, where large-scale food production for export was made profitable by the building of railways from inland areas to the coast and the development of efficient steamships to carry produce across the oceans. The prices of wheat, barley and oats all fell by half between the mid-1870s and the mid-1880s, causing a severe reduction in the income of most colleges which, understandably, they called in aid when contesting the terms of the university contribution. Between 1871 and 1893 the average decline in the external income of all the Cambridge colleges was about 20 per cent; excluding the three biggest colleges – Trinity, King's and Caius – the decline was 40 per cent.[31]

The dividend 'system' was the practice adopted by the colleges of Oxford and Cambridge one by one starting in the sixteenth century, whereby the master and fellows divided amongst themselves the surplus of college income that was left after they had paid the scholars and themselves the sums prescribed in their college statutes, and had paid for the running and maintenance of the college.[32] Since any decision to increase college expenditure, for example, by expanding the numbers of fellows or scholars, paying more to the scholars or paying a contribution to the university, would reduce the surplus to be divided amongst the master and fellows, they had a direct incentive to be ungenerous. The 'capping' of dividends (i.e. the setting of a ceiling), a reform introduced at this time, should have lessened the incentive to fellows to oppose payments to the university: if the surplus were big enough to pay the capped dividend and leave something over, that extra sum could be spent without cutting into the dividend. But the decline in income meant that that rarely happened. At Trinity the loss of income from the agricultural depression, though mild compared with what was suffered by most colleges, was severe enough to prevent for many years a dividend as high as the rather generous figure at which the cap had been set: the cap, expressed in terms of a *modulus* of which the master and other officers got various multiples, was set at £250 in 1882, but for 27 out of the next 34 years (from 1882 to 1916) the modulus had to be fixed at less than £250, which meant that the incentive to be ungenerous was still present.

---

31 J. F. D. Dunbabin, 'Oxford and Cambridge College Finances, 1871–1913', *Economic History Review* 28 (1975): 634.

32 For a brief history of the dividend system see: Robert Neild, *Riches and Responsibility*, 68–74.

At St John's the dividend did not once in those 34 years reach their cap of £250.[33]

The agricultural depression was extremely long and deep. Apart from a short upward blip in the 1914–18 war, food prices remained deeply depressed until the 1939–45 war when protection of agriculture was reintroduced by the government, subsequently to be maintained by the European Union. The depression was so severe that land was abandoned year after year till the arable area of farms in Great Britain, which stood at 18.1 million acres in 1875, had fallen to 11.9 million acres in 1939.[34] In the 1930s the sight of derelict fields and unemployed farmhands was as common as the sight of abandoned factories, closed mines and unemployed industrial workers and miners.

Thus the colleges and university emerged from 30 years of disputes over reform with liberal, democratic statutes (apart from the treatment of women), with improved financial management and accounting, and with the political and financial balance between the colleges and the university adjusted in favour of the university. But from its birth the university's new financial regime was tested by hard times that were to persist for many years.

---

33 I am grateful to Professor Boyd Hilton for this information about St John's.

34 B. R. Mitchell, *British Historical Statistics* (1988), 186–8.

Appendix 1A: The Pay of Trinity's Three Regius Professors

Henry VIII founded five regius professorships in 1540 and subsequently attached three of them – those of Divinity, Greek and Hebrew – to Trinity when he founded it in 1546.[35] (The other two were the regius professorships of Law and Physic.) Trinity's statutes provided that the three professors were not to be fellows of the college with the benefit of free rooms and commons, but were to be paid a stipend of £40 a year. Initially this was good pay compared with that of the fellows, who typically received a stipend, livery allowance and commons worth in total about £10, plus free rooms.[36] But when rapid Tudor inflation eroded the value of money the regius professors were not compensated by the college for the decline in the value of their stipend. If they had been endowed with a parcel of property, or a specified share in Trinity's property, they would have gained from rising rents, but their stipend was set in money.

Compensation came from other sources. In 1605 James I annexed the rectory of Somersham in Huntingdonshire to the regius professorship of Divinity, a benefaction that was reputed to be worth £300 a year in 1717 when Richard Bentley, master of Trinity, was appointed to that professorship.[37] And in 1661 Charles II gave the professors of Hebrew and Greek the privilege of holding a fellowship at a college as well as their chair, a valuable concession since they almost all came from Trinity and now could stay on enjoying, like other fellows, good dividends paid from the college's rising rents, as well as rooms and commons, in addition to their £40 stipend. From 1700 to 1850 only one professor of Hebrew and two professors of Greek came from other colleges.[38]

Further, in 1848 the Ecclesiastical Commissioners prepared, and the Queen assented to, a scheme for increasing the pay of the regius professorships of Hebrew and Greek by appointing them to valuable canonries at Ely.[39] As a result of this surprisingly late act of pluralism the position in 1852 was this:

	Divinity	Greek	Hebrew
Stipend from Trinity	£40	£40	£40
Rectory of Somersham	£1,170		
A canonry at Ely		£600	£600
Total	£1,210	£640	£640

---

35 The five were initially funded by the newly established bishopric of Westminster and were filled by Crown nominees. See Leedham-Green, *A Concise History of the University of Cambridge*, 48.

36 Robert Neild, *Riches and Responsibility*, 62.

37 Clark, *Endowments of the University of Cambridge*, 154; and J. H. Monk, *The Life of Richard Bentley, D. D.* (1833), II: 23.

38 D. A. Winstanley, *Early Victorian England* (1940), 292.

39 Clark, *Endowments of the University of Cambridge*, 154.

The incumbents of all three professorships at this time were fellows of Trinity.

The regius professorship of Greek did not benefit from the canonry for long. Presumably influenced by the Victorian religious revival and by the prospect that professors might no longer be in holy orders, the government told the commissioners whom they had appointed in 1877 to enforce reform at Cambridge that they might, with the concurrence of the Ecclesiastical Commissioners, sever the canonry at Ely from the professorship of Greek and transfer it permanently to 'a professorship of a theological or ecclesiastical character'.[40] Trinity swiftly stepped forward to provide alternative money for the professorship. The college's strong tradition in Greek scholarship may have influenced the decision, but it has been suggested to me that two personal concerns may have weighed with the college. First, that if the incumbent of the chair at that time, Professor B. H. Kennedy (he of that Latin Grammar) lost the canonry, he would be left a pauper with only his £40 from Trinity, an understandable concern since appointments were normally for life and there were then no pensions. Secondly, that if alternative finance were not provided and the chair remained dependent on the income from the canonry, Richard Jebb, a Trinity man not in holy orders who was then professor of Greek in Glasgow, hoping to succeed to the Cambridge chair, would not be able to accept it. Ineligible for the canonry, he could not have afforded it.[41]

Whatever its motivation, the college in 1878 wrote into its revised statutes that, when the professorship of Greek next became vacant, Trinity would provide £500 a year, plus a fellowship and the statutory £40. Soon afterwards the university, at the suggestion of the statutory commissioners, agreed to pitch in, and the Trinity component was reduced to £250, a figure written into the college's revised statutes of 1882. These statutes further provided that the regius professors of Divinity and Hebrew, whether fellows of the college or not, were entitled to rooms in college and commons in addition to their £40. To complete the rearrangement, the university's reformed statutes of 1882 created a new Ely professorship of Divinity to be financed by the canonry.[42]

In another move to reduce inequality in the pay of professors the exceptionally large income of the regius professor of Divinity was cut down to size in 1882 when an Act was passed that disannexed the rectory of Somersham from the office of regius professorship of Divinity and vested it in the university. One half of the revenues were to be assigned to the vicar, the other half to the regius professor. In 1934 the rectory was finally detached

---

40 Oxford and Cambridge Act of 1877 (40 and 41 Vict.).
41 I am indebted to Dr Christopher Stray for these suggestions.
42 *Statutes of the University of Cambridge* (1882), B, XIV.

from the university, along with some but not all of its emoluments (which had probably diminished in value) and vested in the incumbent. Meanwhile the canonry attached to the regius professorship of Hebrew had been switched in 1932 to the regius professorship of Divinity and remained annexed to it until 1940. The canonry was then disannexed and suppressed under an Act which laid down that the cathedral would pay £600 a year towards the stipend of the regius professor of Divinity so long as the election to the professorship was limited to persons in priests orders in the Church of England and that if at any time that limitation was removed the obligation should cease forthwith.[43]

In 1926 when new statutes were introduced the Professor of Greek was still entitled to a fellowship at Trinity but, like the professors of Divinity and Hebrew, he now received his stipend from the university. From Trinity they all three received their statutory £40 and, if not fellows, were put 'in the same position as Fellows with regard to rooms and commons in the College'. In the 2004 statutes their entitlement to rooms was modified, and since then they have been 'in the same position as Fellows with regard to commons, and may, if the Council think fit, be permitted to occupy rooms in College on such conditions as the Council shall determine.'

---

43 Ely Cathedral Canonries Act 1940, *Cambridge University Reporter*, 6 July 1940, 1030.

Appendix 1B: The Number and the Pay of Professors from 1852 to 1920, Excluding the Value of Fellowships

	1852	1871	1882	1920
Divinity – Lady Margaret, 1502	1,855	1,855		trust
Divinity – Regius, 1540	1,209	1,434		trust
Greek – Regius, 1540	640	860		650[44]
Hebrew – Regius, 1540	640	860		a canonry
Civil Law – Regius, 1540	319	583	800	800
Physic (medicine) – Regius, 1540	315	529	700	700
Astronomy – Plumian, 1704	525	491	800	800
Astronomy – Lowdean, 1749	436	458	800	800
Mathematics – Sadlerian, 1701	?	581	850	850
Modern History – Regius, 1724	422	408	800	800
Natural Philosophy – Jacksonian, 1782	412	374	800	500
Law – Downing, 1800	313	466		500[45]
Medicine – Downing, 1800	313	529		300[46]
Geology – Woodwardian, 1728	281	537	700	700
Botany, 1724	259	357	700	700
Anatomy, 1707	247	416	600	vacant
Chemistry, 1702	242	632	850	850 + 200
Moral Philosophy, 1683	195	300	700	700
Mineralogy, 1808	159	335	600	300[47]
Mathematics – Lucasian, 1663	157	677	850	850
Divinity – Norrisian, 1777	100	200		800
Arabic – Sir Thos. Adams, 1632	73	300	700	700
Archaeology – Disney, 1851	30	96		194[48]
Music, 1684	neg.	100		200
Political Economy, 1828[49]	63	300	700	700

(*Continued*)

44 The incumbent held a double fellowship.
45 Plus lodge.
46 Plus lodge.
47 Plus a fellowship at Oriel College, Oxford.
48 Also Brereton Reader in Classics.
49 An ad hom. professorship was given to George Pryme in 1828 when he began lecturing on political economy; a permanent professorship was established in 1863 when he retired.

Continued

	1852	1871	1882	1920
Divinity – Hulsean, 1860		572		600
Zoology and Comparative Anatomy, 1866		360	700	700
Sanskrit, 1867		500	700	700
International Law – Whewell, 1868		500		500
Latin – Kennedy, 1869		183	800	800
Experimental Physics – Cavendish, 1871		500	850	850
Fine Arts – Slade, 1869		357		360
Mechanism and Applied Mechanics, 1875			700	850 + 450
Physiology, 1883			800	800
Pathology, 1883			800	800
Divinity – Ely, 1882				a canonry
Mental Philosophy and Logic, 1896			700	700
Chinese, 1897				200
Ancient History, 1898				700
Agriculture, Drapers 1899				800
Biology, Quick				1,000
Agricultural Botany				700
Astrophysics				nil
German – Schroeder				700
English Literature – King Edward VII				800
Genetics				800
Bio-Chemistry				nil
Italian				467
Naval History				700
French				800
Physics				nil[50]
Aeronautical Engineering – Francis Maud				700

(*Continued*)

---

50 The incumbent, J. J. Thomson, was leaving to become master of Trinity.

Continued

	1852	1871	1882	1920
Arabic – Lord Almoner's				50
Anglo-Saxon – Elrington and Bosworth				500
Ecclesiastical History – Dixie				500
Surgery				600
Total number of professorships	25	32	37	56

Notes: The 1877 commissioners set the maximum at £850. Professors with stipends from the university listed in statute B, chap. VI, schedule C (1882) were subject to a deduction of £200 from their stipend if they held a college fellowship.
Sources: 1852: *Report of the Cambridge University Commission* (1852) 71–3; 1871: *Report of the Royal Commission on Oxford and Cambridge* (1874), I: 136; *Statutes of the University of Cambridge* (1882), 54–5; 1922: *Report of the Royal Commission on Oxford and Cambridge Universities* (1922), Appendices, 148.

Chapter 2

IMPOVERISHMENT

At the turn of the twentieth century the university faced hard times. Between 1883 and 1913 total output in Britain at constant prices increased by nearly 80 percent, a useful rate of growth, though lower than that in Germany, the United States and other countries that had started to industrialise later than Britain (Table 2.1). Prices were approximately stable, but all the growth was in industry and services: the output of British agriculture, the sector in which nearly all the capital of the colleges and university was invested, declined slightly.

There followed the disastrous 1914–18 war, during which inflation was violent, and at the end of which total output and agricultural output were both slightly lower than they had been in 1913.[1]

Table 2.1. Economic indices for the United Kingdom, 1883 to 1920

	1883	1913	1920
Population	100	129	132
GDP at constant prices	100	169	165
Of which:			
Industry	100	177	176
Transport and communications	100	214	199
Distribution and other services	100	174	169
Agriculture	100	98	92
Retail prices	100	100	244
Weekly wage rates	100	119	306
Share prices	100	154	264

Source: C. H. Feinstein, *Statistical Tables of National Income, Expenditure and Output of the U.K. 1855–1965* (1976), Tables 4, 8, 55 and 65; share prices from B. R. Mitchell, *British Historical Statistics* (1988), 688–9.

---

1 The historical statistics used in Table 2.1 and 4.1 were published in the 1970s and later. They were prepared at the Department of Applied Economics at Cambridge, which was created in 1939 on the initiative of J. M. Keynes, as an adjunct of the Faculty of Economics, but did not take off till after the war when Richard Stone was appointed as director.

Table 2.2. Income of the university and colleges, 1883, 1913 and 1920*

	£		
	1883	1913	1920
Colleges			
Endowment income, including trusts	231,000	268,000	288,000
University			
Endowment income	14,000	30,000	55,000
Of which: 'free'	*3,000*	*2,000*	*9,000*
Trust	*11,000*	*28,000*	*46,000*
Fees and dues	30,000	74,000	114,000
Government: Specific grants	0	8,000	23,000
General grants			30,000
Contribution from colleges	5,000	22,000	24,000
University press	0	1,500	0
Other	0	1,000	7,000
University total	50,000	137,000	254,000

* Years to end December.
Sources: 1883 and 1913: Chest income of the university, *Cambridge University Reporter*, 5 March 1884 and 23 March 1914; income of the colleges and the contribution paid to the university, *Report of the Royal Commission on Oxford and Cambridge Universities* (1922), Appendices, 142; trust income of the university from author's summation of individual trusts. 1920: *Report of the Royal Commission* (1922), 196 and Appendices, 329.

The Fate of the Colleges

Between 1883 and 1913, the colleges' endowment income increased a little, helped by the development of some urban land, mostly for residential use; in this respect Oxford did better than Cambridge.[2] Then between 1913 and 1920 the colleges were crushed by the combination of sluggish endowment income, the loss of fees as young men went to the trenches and extreme inflation. Deflated by the increase in wages, the colleges' endowment income in 1920 was only 40 per cent of what it had been in 1883; deflated by the increase in prices, 50 per cent. Since so large a part of college (and university) income was spent on salaries and wages, the figure of 40 per cent is probably the better guide to the severity of the squeeze; either way the loss of real income was huge.

The Lure of Land

At first sight it is remarkable that the colleges and university stayed so largely invested in agricultural land and consequently suffered such acute impoverishment, but one can see several explanations for their behaviour.

2 J. F. D. Dunbabin, 'Oxford and Cambridge College Finances, 1871–1913', *Economic History Review* 28 (1975): 637–8.

In the first place there was the safety of rural and urban land as an income-earning asset for a person or institution. Government bonds had become safe from the risk of default in the eighteenth century, but had been badly devalued by inflation during the Napoleonic Wars and the 1914–18 war; equities, little regulated, were risky; gold and silver were good stores of value but brought no income. Long experience told in favour of holding land, and so did inertia. In the words of Tressilian Nicholas, senior bursar of Trinity from 1929 to 1956, '...at the beginning of the 20th century real property was regarded as the only suitable form of investment for a corporate body'.[3]

Secondly, the master and fellows of the colleges were forbidden by Elizabethan statutes to sell their land lest they do so for their own benefit. Only in 1898 were they allowed in limited conditions to invest in fixed interest securities, subject to government supervision. Further liberalisation came slowly (Appendix 2A).

Thirdly, the dons took pleasure in thinking of themselves as rural landlords. They took pride in the possession of 'foundation land'; they might look forward – or backward – to days spent shooting over a college farm and being entertained to lunch by the tenant. In 1919 the president of Magdalen College, Oxford, when meeting the president of the Board of Education in a deputation to seek government financial aid, opined that 'He thought [the colleges] had administered their estates in a friendly spirit, and had valued easy relations with their tenants, though it had always been a question whether the hand of avarice might not increase income from this source.'[4] Moreover when the dons experienced impoverishment in the agricultural depression they must have felt at one with other landlords. This was the period when aristocratic landowners, desperate to save their estates, married American millionairesses and sold their works of art to Duveen, that larger-than-life dealer who made a fortune buying art treasures from the impoverished *anciens riches* of Europe and selling them to the *nouveaux riches* of the United States.

The Fate of the University

Because the colleges were so severely squeezed, the amount the university received from them under the university contribution scheme introduced in 1882 was disappointing. It had been enacted that the total paid by the colleges should increase in steps to £30,000 at the turn of the century;[5] and

---

3 Speech by Tressilian Nicholas, senior bursar of Trinity College, Cambridge, from 1929 to 1956, at the celebration of his 100th birthday in 1988, *Trinity College Cambridge Annual Record, 1987–88*, 23.

4 *Report of Royal Commission* (1922), Appendices, 222.

5 See Chapter 1.

the figure would probably have been raised further, possibly much further, if the income of the colleges had increased anything like as much as the money GDP (which grew five times between 1883 and 1920). As it was, the colleges on four occasions were granted relief from full payment of the contribution under the hardship clause in the 1882 statutes, and the increase to £30,000 was postponed for six years. Moreover, by 1920 inflation had reduced to half or less the value of the money that was paid by the colleges to the university.

The two ways in which the university could increase its income were by increasing fees and by fund-raising.

The Reform of Fees

As we saw in Chapter 1, student fees, which were charged for matriculation, for degrees, and as a capitation tax, were raised before 1851 to the point where a proposal for further increase was rejected. Nevertheless there was a fivefold increase in revenue from fees between 1851 and 1883 (Table 2.3). This resulted from reforms and increases in fees, and a doubling in student numbers.

Table 2.3. The changing pattern of university fees, 1851 to 1939

	A. Number of students admitted				
	1851	1883	1913	1921	1939
	449	894	1,200	1,821	1,934
	B. The revenue from fees in £				
	1851*	1883	1913	1921	1939
Matriculation	1,874	9,269**	6,390	10,001	8,474
Capitation tax	1,957	9,894	11,819	27,111	26,628
Degrees BA and other	1,835	10,313	13,747	8,680	10,404
Examination fees			12,985	19,918	29,824
Departmental fees			24,768	69,325	157,896
Total of above	5,666	29,466	72,709	135,035	233,226

* The figures are averages for 1845–51.
** Including fees for examinations of unstated amount.
Sources: The number of matriculations (students admitted) is taken from the *Historical Register of the University of Cambridge*. Revenue from fees: 1845–51 from *Royal Commission on the University and Colleges of Cambridge* (1852), 'Evidence from the University', 15–16 and 32–3; other years from the *Cambridge University Reporter*'s annual accounts of the university.

Under the decadent regime inherited from the eighteenth century, students seeking a degree had been obliged to make payments to numerous sinecure officials and servants of the university. These offices were now abolished and the payments to them were replaced by higher payments to the university chest, with the students' money being redirected to proper use. The scale of the former malpractice is remarkable. The following is a list of the payments a student formerly had to make in order to obtain a BA:[6]

Table 2.4. Details of the sums paid for a BA degree before reform

	$£.$	s.	d.
University chest	2	6	1
Registrary	0	4	0
Presenter	0	0	4
2 Scrutators	0	0	8
3 Bedells	0	10	10
Bellringer	0	0	3
2 Proctors	0	14	0
Proctors' servants	0	4	0
2 Proproctors	0	7	0
Proproctors' servants	0	2	0
Marshall	0	0	6
St Mary's Church	0	0	4
Orator	0	1	6
2 Moderators	0	9	0
Government tax [abolished 1868]	3	0	0
Total	8	0	6

The number of persons that had to be paid is astonishing. Moreover this is just one of 35 schedules giving the details of the fees charged for degrees for different categories of candidate that were set out in the university's submission to the royal commission in 1851. The schedules differ according to the degree being taken and the status of the candidate. For the higher degrees, which few people took, the fees were few but sometimes large. One does not know how the sinecurists acquired their posts. In the eighteenth century, nepotism, patronage based on mutual favours, and outright purchase were all normal.[7]

---

6 *Report of Royal Commission on the University and Colleges of Cambridge* (1852), 'Evidence from the University', 32–3.

7 Robert Neild, *Public Corruption: The Dark Side of Social Evolution* (2002), chap. 6 and 7.

The result of reform in the case of charges for a BA was this:[8]

Table 2.5. The cost of a BA degree, 1851 and 1883

	£	
	1851	1883
Paid to		
1. The university chest	2 6 1	7 0 0
2. University officers and servants	2 11 5	Nil
3. Government tax	3 0 0	Nil
4. Other	0 3 0	Nil
Total	8 0 6	7 0 0

Thus in 1883 the student paid one pound less than in 1851 for a BA and the university got nearly five pounds more, three of which came from the ending of the government's stamp duty on degrees, the rest from reform. Of the gain to the university chest, some small part will have gone to pay the reduced staff necessary for the reformed degree ceremonies.

After 1883, two new kinds of fee burgeoned: examination fees and departmental fees. By 1913 they yielded as much as the traditional fees, by 1921, far more.

These new fees were a consequence of the modernisation of the university. Oral exams gave way to more costly written exams for a growing population of students: the number of matriculations doubled again between 1883 and 1921 (Table 2.3). And as the departments in the physical sciences grew they, one after another, introduced departmental fees to cover the costs of the staff, materials and equipment required to teach their subject, costs that differed from subject to subject but generally were substantially higher than those in the arts.

Fund-Raising

As noted in Chapter 1, appeals for money met with some success in the late eighteenth century, but little after the Napoleonic Wars. There was, however,

---

8 It is impossible to be sure that there were no invisible ancillary charges in 1883, but the evidence suggests there were none: I have found none in the university accounts, and the section of *The Student's Guide to the University of Cambridge* for 1882 devoted to 'University and College Expenses', written by the Rev. H. Latham, fellow and tutor of Trinity Hall, lists none, only the fee of £7.

one notable spontaneous gift: Viscount Fitzwilliam, who died in 1816, left his art collection and £100,000 for the building and support of the museum that bears his name. This, like many gifts today, brought to the university not income but a building with valuable contents, in this case works of art. The effect of such gifts is for the university to enjoy benefits in kind that are necessary for teaching and research in, for example, art history or physics; and in the case of the Fitzwilliam Museum and the Botanic Garden the university became responsible for, and embellished by, an institution that brings aesthetic pleasure to the public. But a problem with these, as with all gifts of buildings and similar physical assets, is that the recipient is landed with calls upon future income to finance their maintenance and periodic refurbishment, unless the gift includes a fund for that purpose.

At the end of the nineteenth century the university enjoyed a significant inflow of gifts for the development of the physical sciences thanks very largely, it would seem, to the contributions, direct and indirect, of the two dukes of Devonshire who in succession were chancellor of the university, the seventh duke from 1861 to 1891, the eighth from 1891 to 1908.

In the long era when the development of the physical sciences in England depended heavily on the curiosity, the brains and the patronage of rich men, (in contrast to France, Germany and other European countries where the government backed the development of the sciences) the Cavendish family was outstanding. Henry Cavendish (1731–1810) made important discoveries in many fields and has been described as 'the outstanding natural philosopher of late eighteenth-century Britain' – an accolade indeed.[9] The seventh duke, benefactor of the Cavendish Laboratory, was a Trinity man of high intellectual ability. In 1829 he was 'second wrangler and first Smith's prizeman', meaning that he came second in the mathematical tripos and first in the prize competition for proficiency in mathematics and the physical sciences.[10] Having become a recluse after the early death of his wife, he devoted his life to managing the family estates and to public duties, including the service of Cambridge and other universities, and the promotion of the sciences. He inherited the family's vast estates in 'a condition of unexampled splendour and severe indebtedness', consequent on the sixth duke's extravagant expenditure on the aggrandisement and enjoyment of Chatsworth House, Bolton Castle, Devonshire House in Mayfair (which with its garden ran from Piccadilly back to Berkeley Square)[11] and Lismore Castle in Ireland.[12] To restore the family finances

---

9 Simon Schaffer, 'Cavendish, Henry (1731–1810)', www.oxforddnb.com.
10 F. M. L. Thompson, 'Cavendish, William, seventh duke of Devonshire (1808–1891)', www.oxforddnb.com.
11 See John Rocque's map of London of 1746.
12 David Cannadine, *Aspects of Aristocracy, Grandeur and Decline in Modern Britain* (1994), 171–7.

he invested heavily and with temporary success in the development of Barrow-in-Furness, putting money into the local railway, into steel-making from newly discovered local iron ore, and then, less successfully, into the development of shipbuilding, shipping and jute. A second important enterprise was the development on family land of the seaside resort of Eastbourne. Amongst his public services he was chairman of the Royal Commission on Scientific Instruction and the Advancement of Science, whose third report in 1873 helped to persuade Disraeli to back the reform of Oxford and Cambridge. It was as an earnest of his commitment to the cause of science that he paid for the building of the Cavendish Laboratory with a gift of £6,300 in 1874.[13]

The eighth duke, who in a short stay at Trinity gained a second in maths, was no recluse. He pursued blood sports, racing and gambling – he was one of the Prince of Wales's set – and was an active politician. But, like his father, he actively managed the family fortunes and encouraged technical, scientific, and higher education.[14] In 1899 he agreed to preside over a meeting at Devonshire House to launch, at the suggestion of the university, a Cambridge University Association 'to procure the better endowment of the university'. He and two other rich donors – W. W. Astor Esq. and Messrs N. M. Rothschild – led the way by giving £10,000 each, but the total sum raised by 1902 came to only £70,000.[15] The duke 'discovered that successful businessmen were reluctant to support the university financially, believing that its education was of little relevance to their world.'[16] A few years later an appeal by Oxford was no more successful.[17]

Most of the £70,000 was not restricted as to its use by its donors and was assigned by the Senate to the erection of new buildings and to the creation of an Endowment Fund for their maintenance. Further, it was resolved that 'of any future benefactions, not specifically assigned, at least one quarter shall be transferred to this Endowment Fund'.[18]

13 Thompson, 'Cavendish, William, seventh duke of Devonshire'; and J. W. Clark, *Endowments of the University of Cambridge* (1904), 515.

14 Jonathan Parry, 'Cavendish, Spencer Compton, eighth duke of Devonshire (1833–1908)', www.oxforddnb.com; and Cannadine, *Aspects of Aristocracy*, 177–82.

15 Clark, *Endowments of the University of Cambridge*, 596–608. Here is a complete list of the subscribers to the appeal.

16 Parry, 'Cavendish, Spencer Compton, eighth duke of Devonshire'.

17 J. P. B. Dunbabin, 'Finance and Property', in *The History of the University of Oxford*, ed. M. G. Brock and M. C. Curthoys (1997), VI: 400–1; and *The Oxford Magazine*, 16 October 1913, 10–11.

18 Letter of 24 March 1902 from the vice chancellor, A. W. Ward, to the chancellor, the Duke of Devonshire, Cambridge University Library Archives, UA.FB.22i.

Another notable benefactor was Lord Rayleigh (1842–1919), the physicist and third baron of that title. Having been senior wrangler and won the first Smith's prize in 1865, he was elected a fellow of Trinity College in 1866; but in 1871 he was obliged by the Elizabethan statutes still in force to resign his fellowship in order to marry. (His bride was the sister of his friend A. J. Balfour, the future prime minister.) Fortunately he was rich enough to be able to pursue his researches at the family seat, Terling Place in Essex, where he established a laboratory that he used for the rest of his life. When in 1904 he won the Nobel Prize for Physics he gave the prize money to the university, partly for the Cavendish Laboratory, partly for the university library. From 1908 to 1919 he was chancellor of Cambridge University.

Rayleigh's story illustrates how the rule of celibacy, which was lifted college by college starting only in 1861, could damage the career of a fellow. Fortunately, he was able to escape the choice between his career as a scientist and marriage: he was rich enough to move away and have both. It is sobering to think that Charles Darwin (1809–1882), an undergraduate of Christ's College whom Cambridge claims as one of its greatest sons, would have been ineligible, after he married in 1839, to pursue his studies at Cambridge had he wished to do so. Fortunately he, like Rayleigh, was rich enough to be able to work at home.

Why Elizabeth I imposed celibacy on the colleges of Oxford and Cambridge twelve years after it had been lifted from the church by her father is obscure to me. Diarmaid MacCulloch tells us that amongst her religious preferences, which she prudently concealed but sometimes betrayed, 'she retained a lifelong detestation of married clergy…'[19] Whatever the cause, it is astonishing that this rule of hers lived on into the second half of the nineteenth century.

The Cambridge University Association continued to raise money until the 1950s. After a second general appeal had brought in only £3,000, it was resolved in 1905 to seek money only for specific projects. With this approach they were more successful. In 1904, their first specific appeal brought in £20,000 for improvements to the university library, still in the Cockerell Building, of which £5,000 came from the Goldsmith's Company, £2,700 from Lord Rayleigh's gift and the rest in smaller sums from members of the university. Between 1904 and 1914 several more appeals were launched, and by 1908 the association reckoned it had raised £138,000 (including the initial appeal).[20]

---

19 Diarmaid MacCulloch, *The Later Reformation in England, 1547–1603* (2001), 25. See also Helen L. Parish, *Clerical Marriage and the English Reformation: Precedent Policy and Practice* (2000), 229.

20 *A Short History of the Cambridge University Association*, proof copy, Cambridge University Archives.

The university also received substantial endowments independently of the association. The largest was the gift by Charles Brinsley Marlay, a Trinity man, of his collection of illuminations, manuscripts and a variety of other works of art which came to the Fitzwilliam Museum in 1912, together with nearly £100,000 which Sidney Cockerell, the director of the museum, had persuaded Marlay to give the museum so that it might build an extension to house his collection and be able to pay for its upkeep.

From the scattered data I cannot put a figure on the total value of the gifts received by the university in this period. The increase in the university's income from trusts shown in Table 2.2 is an indication of their magnitude, but it does not reflect the value of the gifts for capital expenditure on new buildings. What is clear is that such increase in its income as the university achieved before the 1914–18 war by fund-raising and by increasing fees charged to students, was to be greatly outweighed by the adverse effects of stagnant endowment income, the loss of fees as young men went to the trenches, and extreme inflation during the war. To continue uncrippled the university needed new money.

Appendix 2A: The Easing of the Constraints on Investments[21]

The Elizabethan constraints on investment were removed in slow steps:

1. In 1856 the colleges and university were allowed to sell their estates and buy other land, subject to the consent and supervision of the Copyhold Commissioners, a government agency that supervised a wide range of transactions relating to land: they were allowed to switch their investments provided they stuck to land.[22]
2. In 1858 they were given scope to benefit from the new demands for land generated by the industrial revolution by introducing mining leases for 60 years and building leases for 99 years.
3. In 1898, after Oxford and Cambridge bursars had jointly urged the Board of Agriculture to ease the constraints on college investments in view of the agricultural depression, the colleges and university were granted freedom to invest part of their foundation assets in financial securities, subject to constraints: the investments had to be made with the consent of the Board of Agriculture, which had now replaced the Copyhold Commissioners, and in their name; and the securities had to be those in which trustees were authorized to invest trust money, which then meant fixed interest securities only.[23] However this last rule could soon be circumvented, since it was ruled after the First World War that, where there was an express investment clause authorising investment in a particular kind or kinds of asset, that clause should be followed, and the constraints in the Trustee Act could be ignored.[24] As to 'free capital', meaning that which had been received in post-foundation bequests or accumulated out of income, the colleges and university were already able as a rule to invest in equities.

No further easing of the investment regime was introduced till 1961, when trustees generally were empowered to invest half their trust funds in stocks and shares, a proportion that was increased to three quarters in 1966.

---

21 Reproduced from: Robert Neild, *Riches and Responsibility: the Financial History of Trinity College, Cambridge* (2008), 87–8.
22 In full, 'The Tithe, Copyhold and Enclosure Commissioners'.
23 *Report of the departmental committee appointed by the Board of Agriculture to inquire into the workings of the Universities and Colleges Estates Acts, 1858 to 1880, and to report whether any, and if so what, amendments therein are desirable*, PP 1897, C.8646; and Universities and Colleges Estates Act 1898, 61 and 62 Vict., chap. 55.
24 Graham Moffat, with Gerard Bean and John Dewar, *Trusts Law: Text and Materials* (2005), 459–60; and A. J. Oakley, *Parker and Mellows: Modern Law of Trusts*, 8th ed. (2003), 603.

In 1964 Ministry of Agriculture supervision was finally removed: colleges and the universities were left free to choose their investments, subject only to the constraints that apply to all charities.[25]

With the notable exception of King's College, much of whose money Keynes put into equities in the 1920s, the colleges, out of caution, inertia, and the plain difficulty of finding buyers for land of little value, did not quickly to take advantage of their freedom.

25 Hubert Picarda, *The Law and Practice Relating to Charities* (1999), 509–11.

Chapter 3

THE GOVERNMENT STEPS IN

The Government Initiative

In early 1917 the president of the Board of Education became convinced that

> Oxford and Cambridge could not continue to discharge their functions or to cope with the developing requirements of applied science without help from the State. Their needs were crying. Without immediate financial aid it would have been impossible for them to carry on their current scientific work. Austen Chamberlain was fortunately Chancellor of the Exchequer. He was an alumnus of Cambridge and the son of the founder of Birmingham University. Few words were necessary to convince such a man of the needs of the two universities. After twenty minutes I left the Treasury Chambers with an assurance of a certain grant of £30,000 a year for each university pending the report of the Royal Commission, which we agreed must necessarily be set up.[1]

The minister who wrote those words was H. A. L. Fisher, an Oxford history don who had been persuaded by Lloyd George to enter Parliament and join his coalition government in 1916. In 1918 he had put through a radical reform of primary and secondary education, and in 1920 he had introduced the first state university scholarships, two hundred of them a year to be shared equally by boys and girls. Now he was to tackle higher education with equal success: His 'delicate balancing of the government's interest in tertiary education and the universities' interest in their own autonomy was something of a triumph.'[2]

The Reactions of Oxford and Cambridge

To impose a royal commission on Oxford and Cambridge was not easy, partly because it was necessary to deal with them together with the new universities

---

1 H. A. L. Fisher, *An Unfinished Autobiography* (1940), 115–16.
2 A. Ryan, 'Fisher, Herbert Albert Laurens (1865–1940)', www.oxforddnb.com.

that had sprouted in the nineteenth century and were already in receipt of some state funding.[3] In November 1918 the two vice-chancellors were invited to join a deputation of the heads of the state-aided universities to see Fisher 'for the purpose of applying to the Government for greatly increased financial support'.[4] But the vice-chancellor of Oxford, the Rev'd H. E. D. Blakiston, president of Trinity College, a man who, according to his biographer, 'can be justly criticized for his snobbishness, his racism, and his anti-feminism', clearly found it difficult to bring himself to be a supplicant of the government, let alone to accept an invitation to line up with his begging bowl alongside representatives of state-aided universities. His reply to Fisher's invitation, dated 19 November 1918, started thus:

> My dear Fisher,
> Your circular letter refers primarily to the state-aided Universities, from which we differ in this matter, first, because we have no funds 'from local sources', and, secondly, because hitherto we have received very little aid from the State, Convocation being (in my opinion rightly) suspicious of Government interference. It would be undesirable in the time at our disposal to attempt to give you the detailed statements of 'requirements' or 'special provisions' which the modern Universities no doubt keep written up from year to year. I can only indicate the lines on which certain subsidies have been given us hitherto and the principles on which further assistance might be accepted.

After some haughty paragraphs in which he rejected the idea of a block grant and proposed 'favourable consideration for applications made to the appropriate Government Departments for facilitating special purposes or promoting special developments', he wrote in his last paragraph:

> I suppose that the speechifying at the deputation will be left to the representatives of the State-aided Universities. But if you like to call upon me, I can say a few words from the point of view indicated above.[5]

From Cambridge the acting vice-chancellor, Thomas C. Fitzpatrick, president of Queens' College, wrote modestly to Fisher on 20 December 1918:

> Dear Sir,
> In view of the statement in your letter to me of 6th November that 'On general grounds I think it would be desirable that the government should

---

3 Gillian Sutherland, 'Education', in *The Cambridge Social History of Britain* (1990), III: 156–7.

4 *Report of the Royal Commission on Oxford and Cambridge Universities* (1922), Appendices, 217.

5 *Report of Royal Commission* (1922), Appendices, 217–18.

obtain a conspectus of the needs of Higher Education over the whole country' I venture to place before you a statement of the financial needs of this University, though it is unofficial and has not been put before the Senate for approval.

Having in several paragraphs explained the needs of the university and having recalled the services its members rendered to the state in many directions during the war, he concluded:

On all these grounds, therefore, it seems not unreasonable in my opinion that the university should receive a substantial grant from the National resources provided that the conditions under which it is given do not interfere with the autonomy to which throughout the long history of the University the Senate has always attached the utmost importance.[6]

From Oxford Blakiston went on being, if not cantankerous, difficult, but the needs of the universities were sufficiently acute and the diplomatic skills of Fisher and his advisers sufficiently great, to ensure that a way forward was soon found. Whereas the government had up-to-date knowledge of the finances of the state-aided universities, it was ignorant of those of Oxford and Cambridge and their colleges. Consequently each of the two old universities was told that the government would provide an emergency grant to keep it going only 'on condition that in due course a comprehensive inquiry into the whole resources of the University and its Colleges, and into the use which is being made of them, shall be instituted by the Government.' Once the inquiry had been made the government would be prepared 'to consider in conjunction with the University, if it so desires, the conditions under which a grant designed to meet the permanent requirement of the University might be made'.[7]

Earlier, at a meeting with Blakiston and other representatives of Oxford, Fisher had explained that the government, at the suggestion of the state-aided universities, had decided that block grants should replace grants made to individual university departments, a change which would 'help to safeguard the autonomy of University administration', and that

Henceforward, practically all the money for university education would be borne on the Treasury Vote, and would be allocated in annual Block Grants determined for a period of five years, after consideration of the

6 *Report of Royal Commission* (1922), Appendices, 224.
7 *Report of Royal Commission* (1922), Appendices, 226.

recommendations of a single Standing Committee appointed by the Chancellor of the Exchequer on the recommendation of the President of the Board of Education, the Secretary of State for Scotland, and the Chief Secretary for Ireland.[8]

Thus did Fisher announce the creation of the University Grants Committee (the UGC), composed of ten academics under an independent chairman, to allocate money which, exceptionally, was voted to it for five years at a time, not one year. It seems that the Treasury for constitutional reasons insisted that the money should be administered directly from the Treasury, and that Fisher backed the creation of a committee of academics to guide the Treasury as a means of preventing future interference by the Board of Education in the universities.[9] The Treasury's case was that 'Since the Committee to administer the grants was to be one for the whole United Kingdom, it had to be appointed by one authority with jurisdiction for the three kingdoms. The writ of the Board of Education ran only to England and Wales. Therefore it had to be the Treasury which appointed the Committee....'[10] We shall discuss later how well the UGC performed.

The UGC, besides making recurrent grants, the spending of which was wholly at the discretion of the universities, made non-recurrent grants for capital expenditure, maintenance and the like, the allocation of which in response to competing applications inevitably gave them some influence over the pace and shape of the evolution of the universities.[11] In 1919 the total grant of approximately £1 million went two-thirds to recurrent, one third to non-recurrent grants.

The Third Royal Commission

As a result of Fisher's exertions, a royal commission on Oxford and Cambridge universities was appointed in November 1919. Asquith, the former prime minister, now Lord Oxford, was to be chairman, and many distinguished academics were to be members. Unusually, it was designed and 'authorised to sit' in three parts: an Oxford Committee, a Cambridge Committee and

---

8 Record by Mr Fisher's secretary of the meeting on 15 May 1919, *Report of Royal Commission* (1922), Appendices, 221.

9 See Tom Owen, 'The University Grants Committee', *Oxford Review of Education* 6, no. 3 (1980): 258; and Eric Ashby and Mary Anderson, *Portrait of Haldane at Work on Education* (1974), 152.

10 Tom Owen, 'The University Grants Committee', 258.

11 Robert O. Berdahl, *British Universities and the State* (1959), 58–9.

a Committee on Estates Management. The members of the Cambridge Committee were:

1. Gerald William Balfour (chairman), former fellow of Trinity College, brother of A. J. Balfour;
2. Arthur Henderson, leading moderate Labour politician;
3. Sir Walter Morley Fletcher, biologist, former fellow of Trinity College, secretary of the Medical Research Council;
4. Sir Horace Darwin, civil engineer and manufacturer of scientific instruments at Cambridge, son of Charles Darwin;
5. George Macaulay Trevelyan, historian and later master of Trinity College;
6. Hugh Kerr Anderson, master of Gonville and Caius College, scientist and a leading university administrator;
7. Blanche Athena Clough, principal of Newnham College;
8. Montague Rhodes James, provost of Eton, former provost of King's College, scholar and writer of ghost stories;
9. Sir Arthur Schuster, physicist and foreign secretary of the Royal Society.

The Committee on Estates Management included experts from the world of land surveying and estate management.

This time the government was not inhibited in setting the terms of reference. The commission from the monarch read:

> We have deemed it expedient that a commission should forthwith issue to consider the applications which have been made by the Universities of Oxford and Cambridge for financial assistance from the State and for this purpose to enquire into the financial resources of the Universities and the Colleges and Halls therein, into the administration and application of these resources, into the government of the Universities, and into the relations of the Colleges and Halls to the Universities and to each other, and to make recommendations.[12]

Further, the commissioners were given the power to call before them anyone they thought might yield relevant information; to 'call for such books, documents, registers or records as may afford you the fullest information'; and to visit and inspect such places as they might deem it expedient to inspect.

But the mandate was limited in one important respect. The commission was not invited to consider the curriculum of the universities, a point which Fisher had made in his exchanges with the vice-chancellors. 'The State,'

---

12 *Report of Royal Commission* (1922), 3–4.

he had written, 'is, in my opinion, not competent to direct the work of education and disinterested research which is carried on by Universities, and the responsibility for its conduct must rest solely with their Governing Bodies and Teachers.'[13]

The Commissioners' Analysis

The report of the royal commission started with a lucid 16-page history of the universities from the earliest times to 1882, the end of the great period of reform. It concluded thus:

> The prevailing idea of the legislators of 1850–82 was to raise the intellectual level by free competition. In this they succeeded, to the great advantage of Universities and nation, and in particular to the particular advantage of the cleverest sons of professional men of small means... Nevertheless the Commissioners may perhaps have paid too little attention to the way in which open competition might detrimentally affect some of the more distinctively poor and those educated on other than public school lines. Oxford, however, in 1868, and Cambridge in 1869 re-established the Non-Collegiate system, chiefly for the benefit of poorer men... During the last generation there has been a rapid rise in the number and proportion of students of moderate and even of very slender means, and there are not a few cases nowadays of students with no independent means at all.[14]

The report then analysed developments since 1882. The main points made were:

1. In contrast to the eighteenth century, dons were now conscientious teachers and '*most* [my italics] of the undergraduates [were] now serious and hard-working students, if not entirely divested on all occasions of the exuberance natural to congregated youth' (26).
2. The students were no longer, as in 1852, mainly designed for the church and school masters, but were destined for all the professions, for the public services, and to an increasing degree for business. Many, having been selected for their general ability and having benefited from the improved teaching, were to 'rise to leading positions in very various departments of

---

13 *Report of Royal Commission* (1922), Appendices, 221.
14 *Report of Royal Commission* (1922), 25.

life' (25–26). In other words, the reformed universities were supplying the elite to run the considerably reformed nation.

3. Student numbers had greatly increased – threefold at Cambridge between 1850 and 1912 – and new subjects had been developed, in particular, science at Cambridge (27 and 33).

4. The universities had shown their value to the nation in the war. From the very beginning of the war 'they were almost entirely depleted not only for the fighting but for the thinking services of the Crown.' Oxford and Cambridge gave to the country a peculiarly large number of men fitted to act as officers, and men whose training in languages, pure and applied science, or economics specially fitted them to grapple with new and totally unexpected problems calling for rapid solution (47).

The royal commission put the economic case for government aid tersely: 'Owing to the change in the value of money Oxford and Cambridge are no longer able to pay their way.' The increase in the number of students, in the amount of teaching given to each, and in the variety of subjects in which teaching and research were conducted had necessitated a great increase in staff and expenditure. That had created a serious financial situation before the war: staff had been underpaid and overworked; not a few had had no pension prospects; research, especially in the humanities, was very poorly provided for; and there was difficulty in staffing the libraries and museums. 'If these problems were present before the war, they have been rendered insoluble by the change in the value of money; but for the interim grant of £30,000 a year granted by the State to each University it would have been impossible to continue their present work even provisionally... The present financial position, if unrelieved, must destroy the special value of Oxford and Cambridge to the nation, which lies in their ability to supply the highest type of intellect and training' (48).

The report considered alternative 'ways of obtaining immediate financial relief on a sufficient scale'. Having concluded that to rely on increased fees would tend to turn Oxford and Cambridge into 'rich men's universities', and that university taxation of colleges to a great extent transfers control over money rather than tapping new sources, it turned to private benefactions about which it said:

Private Benefaction. – Here lies the real hope of future prosperity and development for the Universities. The public grant that we propose is, in our opinion, the minimum that is necessary to prevent immediate decline, and is utterly insufficient for future development. There is unfortunately no prospect of private benefactions being obtained sufficiently soon and in sufficient quantity to avert the necessity of such a public grant. This is partly because present conditions, including high taxation and prices, are very unfavourable to private benefaction. The failure of the Oxford women's Colleges to obtain a sufficient response to their appeal is a case in point.

Another reason for the insufficiency of private benefactions is more general and does not apply to the post-war period only. It lies in the relative indifference of our countrymen to the value of education.

Both Universities have indeed gratefully called our attention to generous benefactions which they have received of recent years. But generally speaking there is no such strong tradition of practical gratitude to the Alma Mater as is the just pride of American Universities. We do not regard the State Grant which we are recommending as a substitute for this spirit of private generosity. That spirit must be evoked in academic matters to a much greater extent, if the Empire is to hold its own in the modern world, either in industry or in the higher aspects of education. Since it must be done, we believe that it will be done; but it is yet to do. (54)

The ambivalence is remarkable. First, 'Here lies the real hope', then a recitation of the reasons why there is little hope, and then 'Since it must be done, we believe it will be done.' It is as if a rainmaker said, 'Since we must have rain, we shall have rain, but rain has yet to be made.' The commissioners must have had conflicting considerations in mind: the hope that private benefactions would help to finance development and preserve the independence of the universities; on the other hand, the desire urgently to advocate government aid without suggesting either that the government would have to provide ever more money or that the universities would be able in the future to do without government money. Fisher, when commending to the House of Commons the provision of government money for Oxford and Cambridge, said, with judicious ambiguity as to the future,

> ...when I recall the fate of the appeals which were made by the late Duke of Devonshire on behalf of Cambridge, and by Lord Curzon on behalf of Oxford – and Lord Curzon is very vigorous when he takes on an appeal of this kind – when I remember the fate of those appeals, I realise that it is quite impossible at the present juncture for the two universities to go on doing the work which they are doing, and which they ought to do, without assistance from the state.[15]

---

15 The second reading of the Oxford and Cambridge Universities Bill, House of Commons, 22 June 1923, *Parliamentary Report*, col. 1897–8.

In the discussion of the purposes for which money should be provided, better pay and pension provision for teachers came first: if it were not provided, 'the type of teacher must decline' (48).

> Each University must be placed in a position to offer to all those who do its work a salary and pension prospects enabling a man to marry and bring up a family, with amenities and advantages of education like those of other professional families. (49)

The commission had received submissions from the two universities and from their constituent departments pleading for money for particular needs but, following the view taken earlier by Fisher, it recommended that a round sum should be paid annually, and the universities 'left to apportion it in detail, paying due regard to the views which we have expressed on the question of priority of claims' (215).

The Commissioners' Recommendations

The operational statement with which the commissioners concluded the main report nevertheless included some guidance as to priorities (57):

> We recommend that each University receive, instead of the existing interim grant of £30,000, an annual grant of £100,000 a year, in addition to £10,000 a year for special purposes (Women's education and Extra-Mural work), and a lump sum for pension arrears, in order to enable them to fulfil their functions to the nation in a satisfactory manner.
>
> The principal purposes for which we recommend a grant of public money are as follows:
>
> Proper salaries and pensions for University teachers, which should be a first charge on any public grant; secondly, the adequate maintenance of the University Libraries and Museums; the endowment of research and advanced teaching, including more Professors, Readers and University or Faculty Lecturers, and more research Studentships for young graduates; the most pressing needs of maintenance in respect of Laboratories and departmental Libraries, as part of the apparatus for teaching and research; and the provision at both Universities of a Sites and Buildings Fund (it will be noted that for reasons of public economy we do not recommend a grant of capital moneys for buildings); we also budget for needs of the Non-Collegiate bodies, for a grant towards women's education, and for aid for the extra-mural work of the Universities and for adult education.

The royal commission made a number of recommendations as to the government of the universities; the organisation of teaching and research, the improvement of access for poor candidates through changes in scholarship arrangements and through more efficient catering and cheaper rooms; and similar matters not directly related to finance. As regards finance, it made two notable recommendations: that the formula for university contribution at Cambridge be changed from a flat-rate tax to a graduated tax on college income akin to that at Oxford, rising to a maximum of 10 per cent on net revenue above £10,000; and that the period that must elapse before the terms of a trust could be altered be changed to 60 years from its creation. (Under the existing Act of 1877, only trusts that were than more 50 years old in 1877 could be altered, with the result that the required lapse of time grew longer year by year.)

The report of the Estates Committee is remarkable for what it did not say. This was the time when in the United States, and to a lesser extent in Britain, investment in equities was becoming highly profitable, albeit highly risky, and Keynes was about to start a successful portfolio of equities for King's College. Yet the committee never touched the subject of equities and seems from its name, 'Committee on Estates Management', and its composition, to have been designed not to do so. But the case is odd. The report of the committee starts by saying that their terms of reference instructed them 'to enquire into the financial resources' of the two universities and their colleges, implying that they were invited to look at all types of financial resources. But they go on immediately to renounce enquiry into everything but land. The reasons they give are:

1. The internal revenues, (fees etc.) are a question for consideration by all the members of the royal commission, not by their committee.
2. External investment other than land 'is controlled by the Ministry of Agriculture, whose approval is necessary in any selection or change of investment. We have therefore confined our attention to the financial resources derived from land.'

To refrain from discussing investment in assets other than land in deference to a government department that supervised land transactions but had no expertise in investment policy was to curtail the field of enquiry in a manner that seems inconsistent with the full execution of the royal commission's mandate. Perhaps it was advisable so to act. An unconstrained debate about investment policy into which Keynes would probably have thrown brilliant but controversial proposals for investment in equities might have hindered the chances of getting political support for government money for the universities.

Critics might have said that a government grant would be used for risk-taking.

The Estates Committee made two recommendations of interest. First, that land should be sold and the proceeds put into long-dated securities if that would substantially improve income, though it also offered the qualification, which today is rather baffling: 'That the retention of some land is a useful asset in the corporate life of a College, and should afford that training in practical affairs which is particularly valuable to an educational body.'

Secondly, it proposed

That a map be drawn up showing the land in and near Oxford and Cambridge which is owned by the Colleges and is available for the future development of the Universities. Such Map to be deposited in charge of University Officials, and to show the position and extent of the lands, with the dates at which they next come into hand. (Para. 177)

and

That the Ministry of Agriculture, on the representation of the University, have power to make Provisional Orders, which would be subject to confirmation by Parliament, conferring on the University compulsory powers of acquiring from Colleges and outside owners land which can be shown to be essential to its development for educational purposes. (Para. 178)

The proposal for powers of compulsory purchase was not implemented in the Act that followed. Maps were made of the surrounding lands at this time, but they may not have been a consequence of the Estate Committee's suggestion.

Again, a statutory commission was appointed to apply the recommendations, and in 1926 new university statutes were enacted.[16] As regards the governance of the university the most important change was that only MAs resident in Cambridge, now called the members of the Regent House, could henceforth vote on major policy proposals. Non-resident MAs who, coming from far and wide, had frequently obstructed proposals for reform, remained members of the Senate but were disenfranchised except for the election of the chancellor and high steward, and for approving various ceremonial

---

16 Universities of Oxford and Cambridge Act 1923 (13 and 14 Geo. 5 Chap. 33); and 'Statutes of the University of Cambridge, 1926', in *Statutes of the University of Cambridge and Passages from Acts of Parliament relating to the University* (1928).

graces. Power was now in the hands of those engaged in teaching, research and administration.

As regards finance, the recommendation that the formula for the university contribution should be graduated was followed. Student fees, instead of being allotted course by course, were pooled so that, along with the Treasury grant, they helped to produce a pool from which the pay, pensions and workload of the dons could be improved generally. Financial management was strengthened by the creation of the Treasurer, an officer of the university responsible to the Financial Board. The formula for electing four college-appointed members of the Financial Board, under which votes had been given to colleges according to their income, was changed to one college one vote. A proposal that government representatives might serve on the Financial Board and the General Board of the Faculties was rejected.

The response of governments of the inter-war years to the Asquith recommendation for financial support was remarkably favourable. Although this was the period of the Geddes Axe when public expenditure was being cut severely, the block grant to Cambridge was introduced and raised in steps to £93,500 in 1925–26, a figure little short of the recommended £100,000 and probably of greater value since prices had fallen.

The Introduction of Research Grants

A development no less important than the introduction of the block grant administered by the UGC was the introduction of government research grants and the creation of autonomous councils to administer them. Until the turn of the twentieth century the state had done little to support scientific research. Its main contributions had been to create the Greenwich Observatory in 1675, to maintain a few weapons establishments and, since 1850, to provide a grant for the Royal Society.

The first subject now to gain substantial support was agriculture. Towards the end of the nineteenth century there was a wave of support from landowners and the government for more agricultural education and research.[17] In 1889 the Board of Agriculture was created and began to distribute grants, with some money also provided by local authorities.

The university at first jibbed at accepting these offers. The whole subject of agricultural education was opposed on the grounds that the university did not engage in vocational training. Nevertheless in 1893 a diploma examination, open to outsiders as well as members of the university and

---

17 Paul Brassley, 'Agricultural science and education', in *The Agrarian History of England and Wales*, vol. 7 (1), ed. E. J. T. Collins (2000), 595–640.

subsidised by local authorities, was introduced as an appendage of the university. It did not attract many candidates. However matters changed at the turn of the century when the university's move into agriculture was driven forward by two forces. First, in the late 1890s it accepted from private benefactors a lectureship in agriculture and a professorship. Having thus embraced agriculture as a respectable subject, it gained grants from the Board of Agriculture so successfully that in the following decades it became a major centre of agricultural research, as well as a provider of advice to farmers.[18] Secondly, a one-year course on the rudiments of agriculture was introduced 'in hope of attracting the many undergraduates destined to own and manage estates'.[19] Sons of landowners with modest intellectual aims were thus enabled to get a pass degree (inferior to an honours degree) by passing a Special Exam (meaning an exam that was specially easy) on farming, and passing similar Special Exams on two arts subjects. Based on this curious combination of scientific research and education for gentlemen, the Cambridge School of Agriculture became one of the largest, if not the largest, recipient of the government's agricultural grants, with strength in plant breeding, animal nutrition and a variety of other subjects.

The second subject to get substantial government support was medicine, but here again there was opposition to taking a grant, in this case lest it compromise the independence of the university. In particular, J. J. Thomson feared that inspection would be introduced and might be extended to other scientific departments.[20] After a debate, the taking of medical grants was approved in 1914 by a vote of only 267 to 235.[21] But in the inter-war years the amount of government money received for medical research was small. Another source of government money was the Department of Scientific and Industrial Research (DSIR) which was created in 1915 and given much money to be spent on reducing the wartime dependence of British industry on German products. It was continued in peacetime, but at Cambridge neither it nor medical grants came close to rivalling the amount of money received for agriculture in the inter-war years.

I have been able to assess only approximately how much Cambridge received by way of these government grants in this period. They are entered in such a variety of ways in the accounts of so many university departments

---

18 The Gilbey Lectureship of Agriculture of 1896 and the Drapers' Professorship of 1899.

19 Sir Frank Engledow, 'Agricultural Teaching at Cambridge 1984–1955', Memoir 22 in *University of Cambridge School of Agriculture Memoirs* (1955), 5.

20 J. P. R. Roach, *A History of the County of Cambridge and the Isle of Ely* (1959), III: 273.

21 *Cambridge University Reporter* (1913–14), 57–8 and 753.

that it is hard to know if one has found them all and if one has added them without double-counting. My results are these:

Table 3.1. Government research grants received, 1912–13 to 1945–46

	£	Per cent for agriculture
1912–13	7,600	70
1920–21	27,000	69
1938–39	72,000	83
1945–46	138,000	75

The dominance of agriculture is remarkable.

The Haldane Report

At the end of the 1914–18 war government policy towards the funding of research was given shape by the Haldane Report on the machinery of government of December 1918.[22] Haldane, that remarkable liberal philosopher-politician, having spent time in Germany and seen the advance of higher education and science in that country was much concerned with improving higher education in Britain and played a leading part in the creation of Imperial College in 1907.[23] His report recommended that for the sake of academic independence funds for general research (as distinct from research into specific policy problems commissioned by the government) should be the responsibility not of government departments but of the Lord President of the Council, since he 'is in normal times free from any serious pressure of administrative duties, and is immune from any suspicion of being biased by administrative considerations against the application of the results of research'. In fulfilment of this recommendation, research councils, free from political and administrative pressures, were created under royal charter, starting with the Medical Research Council (MRC) in 1920 to replace the Medical Research Committee. The Agricultural Research Council (ARC) followed in 1931. Money now flowed to the university from these councils as well as directly

---

22 See *Ministry of Reconstruction: Report of the Machinery of Government Committee* (Haldane; Cd 9230, 1918), 34; *Report of the Committee of Enquiry into the Organisation of Civil Science* (Trend; Cmnd 2171, 1963), 30.

23 H. C. G. Matthew, 'Haldane, Richard Burdon, Viscount Haldane, 1856–1928', www.oxforddnb.com; and Richard Burdon Haldane, *An Autobiography* (1929), 91–2 and 139–47.

from government departments and through other intermediaries. Haldane's approach became transmogrified into 'the Haldane principle' and lived on unchallenged until the 1970s.[24]

Conclusion

After the 1914–18 war, government money was provided to the universities via agencies that were dominated by academics, not by representatives of the interested government department – the UGC to administer the block grant, the research councils the research grants. The creation of these bulwarks against intervention in the universities owes much to two remarkable men, Fisher and Haldane. Both were intellectuals imbued with the values of that liberal moment, both were drawn into politics more by duty than ambition.

---

24 The principal challenge came in a report by Lord Rothschild who advocated that in the making of government grants emphasis be given to the prospective commercial fruits of research projects. The implication that research without predictable fruits should come second did not go unchallenged. *A Framework for Government Research and Development* (1971), 17–19.

Chapter 4

THE INTER-WAR YEARS AND THE 1939–45 WAR

The Economic Depression

Between the wars economic depression and mass unemployment hit Britain in two spasms, each followed by a partial recovery. In the aftermath of the 1914–18 war the authorities squeezed the economy so severely that from 1920 to 1921 real gross domestic product (GDP) fell by 10 percent and unemployment rose from 2 to 11 per cent – an astonishingly large collapse in one year. Unemployment then eased a little, but in the slump that followed the Wall Street Crash of 1929 it soared to nearly 16 per cent in 1932. After a partial recovery, it stood at just over 9 per cent in 1938. The national level of wage rates was reduced by 30 per cent between 1920 and 1923 and remained depressed.

Nevertheless real GDP rose by 36 per cent between the wars: technical progress and investment in new industries that were mostly located in the south of England caused the productivity of those in employment to continue upward; and agriculture made some progress (Table 3.1).

The University Recovers

In these economic conditions the finances of the university and the colleges improved. The money income of the university nearly doubled between 1920 and 1939, and there was a gain from lower prices, but not from lower wage rates: wages were reduced heavily in the north of Britain and Wales where the depressed industries – coal-mining, steel, heavy industries and textiles – were concentrated, but less so in the south. A look at the accounts of a few Cambridge colleges shows that the wage rates they paid in 1938 were approximately the same as in 1920, or higher. Adjusted for changes in costs, the university's income probably more than doubled between the wars, having, as we saw in the last chapter, been reduced to half or less by the 1914–18 war.

Table 4.1. Economic indices for the United Kingdom, 1920 to 1946

	1920	1938	1946
Population	100	109	112
GDP at constant factor cost	100	136	143
Of which:			
Industry	100	162	166
Transport and communications	100	145	165
Distribution and other services	100	117	125
Agriculture	100	120	133
Retail prices	100	63	97
National wage rates	100	72	117
Share prices	100	116	160

Source: C. H. Feinstein, *Statistical Tables of National Income, Expenditure and Output of the U.K. 1855–1965* (1976), Tables 8, 55, 57 and 65; share prices from B. R. Mitchell, *British Historical Statistics* (1988), 688–9.

Table 4.2. Income of the university and colleges, 1920, 1939 and 1946

	£ thousands		
	1920	1939	1946
Colleges			
Endowment income, including trusts	288	433	525
University			
Endowment income	55	139	275
Fees	114	235	89
Government general grant	30	121	257
Research grants etc., mostly govt	23	72	154
Contribution from colleges	24	41	54
Other	7	3	20
Total	253	611	849
Government as per cent of total	*21%*	*32%*	*48%*

Source: 1920 from *Report of the Royal Commission on Oxford and Cambridge Universities* (1922), 196 and Appendices, 329; other years from annual university accounts, the *Cambridge University Reporter*, plus income of the colleges from annual reports of the Cambridge University Association (CUA) Financial Board, Min. II.

The extra income came mostly from three sources: fees, the government and gifts:

a. Fees: The amounts charged for matriculation, degrees and capitation tax were now unchanged, but there was a big increase in income from departmental fees for teaching.

b. Government grants: As noted in Chapter 3, the Asquith committee's recommendation of a regular grant of £100,000 a year was fulfilled with some delay: from the mid-1920s onwards the university regularly received money of that order from the UGC. Research grants grew from 9 per cent of total income in 1920 to 16 per cent in 1946. About 90 per cent of this money came directly or indirectly from the government; the rest came from grants and research contracts from the private sector. It is remarkable that 70 per cent or more of the total grants went to agricultural research in each of the years shown. The biggest sums went to animal nutrition, animal pathology and, in 1945–46, to advice to farmers. Substantial sums also went to plant breeding, horticulture and milk testing.

c. Gifts: The university's endowment income other than government grants doubled between 1920 and 1939, mainly as a result of an inflow of new gifts (including legacies). It is not possible to give precise figures because of the lack of consolidated figures for trusts, but by piecing together various data one can see the shape of what happened.

The Inflow of Gifts

Until the end of the nineteenth century gifts were relatively few and simple. They usually endowed professorships and other teaching posts, scholarships and prizes, and a few particular facilities, for example, the university library. In the first half of the twentieth century the pattern was different: the endowment of professorships and other posts continued but there were also big gifts for buildings and equipment for the physical sciences and engineering; and the money came no longer from patrician benefactors so much as from individuals or companies whose money came from the new science-based industries. So much is evident from Table 3.3, which lists gifts worth £20,000 or more recorded in the university archives.[1]

Oil, chemicals, motors and engineering are prominent.

The Cambridge University Association continued to raise substantial sums by specific appeals, but one cannot say what proportion of the total inflow was the result of its efforts. One can see from Table 4.4 that before the 1914–18 war the London Committee of the association was composed of grand, mostly titled, persons and included no industrialists; and that 19 of its 27 members were from Trinity. After the war it included a few industrialists and several bankers.

One may wonder whether the grandeur of the committee's members increased or diminished its ability to attract money from the new industrialists.

---

1 See the typescript in the university archives (unlisted) in which J. W. Clark's work, *The Endowments of the University of Cambridge* (1904) has been carried forward to 1959.

Table 4.3. Gifts worth £20,000 or more, 1908 to 1956

		£ thousands
1908 Sir William Dunn	Biochemistry	210
1912 Arthur Balfour	Genetics (prof.)	20
1912 Marlay Fund	Fitzwilliam Museum	80 and collections
1918 Vere Harmsworth	Naval history	20
1919 Burmah and other oil companies	Chemistry	210
1919 ICI	Engineering	50
1919 Francis Mond (nickel)	Aeronautical engineering (prof.)	20
1919 An Italian	Italian (prof.)	20
1922 Rouse Ball	Maths (prof.)	25
1922 Rouse Ball	Law	25
1923 Rockefeller	Pathology	130
1926 Laura S. Rockefeller	Political science (prof.)	30
1928 John Humphrey Plummer	Physical sciences	100
1928 Rockefeller (I.E.B.)	Library, zoology etc.	700
1930 Montagu Burton	Industrial relations (prof.)	20
1935 Cory Fund	Botanical garden	Annuity of 10+
1936 Sir Herbert Austin (motors)	Physics	250
1944 Institute of Electrical Engineering	Electrical engineering (prof.)	71
R. S. Whipple	Science	25
1945 Shell	Chemical engineering (prof. +)	435
1947 T. C. Beebe	Medicine	40
1948 Fairhaven	Fitzwilliam Museum	30
1949 Ernest Oppenheimer	Chemistry/metallurgy	30
1952 Brooks	Botany	20
1956 Judith B. Wilson	Poetry and drama (lectureship)	30

The desire of the newly rich to associate with the already rich cannot have been altogether dormant. On the other hand, when it came to raising big money for the new university library in 1929 the London Committee, as we shall see below, delegated the task to a committee chaired by and bearing the name of Lord Melchett, whose fortune had come recently from the chemical industry.[2]

---

2 Whereas the Cambridge Association papers relating to appeals generally refer simply to the London Committee, in this case they refer to 'London Committee (Lord Melchett)'. No explanation is given. Lord Melchett created ICI by embracing other firms into the fold of Brunner Mond and Co., the highly successful firm that had been built up by his father, the inventive chemist Ludwig Mond, and his business partner John Brunner.

Table 4.4. The membership of the London Committee of the CUA in 1911

The Right Hon. Lord Rayleigh, OM, ScD, Trinity College (Chairman), Chancellor
of the University

His Grace the Duke of Devonshire, KG, MA, Trinity College (Vice-Chairman)

The Right Hon. the Earl of Crewe, KG, MA, Trinity College

The Right Hon. Earl Carrington, KG, GCMG, MA, Trinity College

The Right Hon. the Earl of Lytton, MA, Trinity College

The Right Hon. the Earl of Plymouth, MA, St John's College

The Right Hon. Viscount Esher, GCB, GCVO, MA, Trinity College

The Right Hon. The Lord Chief Justice, MA, Trinity College

The Right Hon. Lord Kinnaird, MA, Trinity College

The Right Hon. Lord Tennyson, GCMG, MA, Trinity College

The Right Hon. Lord Rothschild, GCVO, MA, Trinity College

The Right Rev. the Lord Bishop of Ely, DD, Queens' College

The Right Hon. Lord Justice Kennedy, MA, Pembroke College

The Right Hon. The Speaker, MA, MP, Trinity College

The Right Hon. A.J. Balfour, MA, MP, Trinity College

The Right Hon. Alfred Lyttelton, MA, MP, Trinity College

Professor Sir Joseph Larmor, MP, Secretary of the Royal Society, St John's College

Sir Richard Solomon, KCMG, MA, Peterhouse

Marlborough R. Pryor, MA, Trinity College

R. C. Lehmann, MA, Trinity College

F. Leverton Harris, MA, Gonville and Caius College

H. C. Gooch, MA, Trinity College

J. J. Withers, MA, King's College

Edwin Freshfield, Junior, MA, Trinity College

A. C. Cole, MA, Trinity College

T. H. Middleton, MA, St John's College

J. F. P. Rawlinson, MA, KC, MP, Trinity College (Hon. Secretary)

It is clear that philanthropy without expectation of commercial gain lay behind two of the largest gifts – and no doubt others that were not so large. The largest was the gift to Cambridge of £700,000 in 1928 by the Rockefeller family. Having been much criticised for the ruthless methods by which they achieved monopolistic command of America's petroleum supplies and an unequalled fortune, the Rockefellers worked to redeem their reputation by philanthropy on an unparalleled scale, mostly directed to education and health.

The Rockefeller Gift

A large part of the Rockefeller gift went, after lengthy negotiations with the university, to help finance the building of the present university library. In May 1921 the university decided that a new building on a new site was needed for the library, which had long been crippled by inadequate space in the

Old Schools.[3] In 1925 more than seven acres were purchased from Clare and King's colleges, in a transaction of some complexity that is described in the Chapter 5. Plans were prepared that envisaged the raising of a capital sum of £500,000 to finance the construction of a building designed by Sir Giles Gilbert Scott, and to provide for its subsequent staffing and maintenance. In March 1928 it was agreed that the university should find half that sum (£250,000). Of this, £25,000 was to come from the Local Examinations Syndicate, £65,000 from a recent bequest of the Rev. John Henry Ellis of Trinity, and the remainder was to be raised through a loan to be repaid over 50 years.

At this stage the International Education Board, an educational charity created in 1923 by John D. Rockefeller, Junior, indicated that it would be prepared to consider a comprehensive gift to Cambridge 'to cover the needs of agriculture, biology and certain allied sciences lying within a region specified by them, and the need for a new Library.' Negotiations were held between the International Education Board and the university, which appointed as its representative Sir Hugh Anderson, master of Gonville and Caius, who had been a leading member of the Asquith royal commission that reported in 1922. The result was a grand plan for a capital outlay of no less than £1,179,000, made up as follows:[4]

	£
Library	500,000
Zoology	168,000
Agriculture	163,000
Biophysics	122,000
Botany	108,000
Physiology	88,000

The International Education Board agreed to provide £700,000 if the University provided the remaining £479,000. Since the university had already committed £250,000, it needed to raise the final £229,000. The main sources from which this further sum was raised were:

	£
The government (Ministry of Ag. and Fish)	50,000
The Empire Marketing Board	50,000
The Royal Agricultural Society	1,000

---

3 University Grace 2 of 7 May 1921.

4 These allocations were later changed slightly since the Plummer bequest, listed above, partially met one of the needs.

$£$

Cambridge University Association:	
a. London Committee (Lord Melchett)	60,000
b. Cambridge Committee	31,000
c. Cambridge University Press	12,000
Total	204,000

Work on the new library was started in 1931 and it was opened by George V in October 1934, when new buildings for agriculture, botany, physiology and zoology funded by the scheme were also open for inspection. One cannot but speculate as to why Scott crowned his design with the gross tower of industrial style that dominates the skyline of Cambridge. Maybe he, the architect of Battersea Power Station, was seeking, perhaps unconsciously, to outdo his grandfather, who had designed the lumpy tower of St John's chapel that not long before had been thrust into the skyline.

The second and rather unusual case of apparently pure philanthropy is the bequest of £210,000 for biochemistry that came from Sir William Dunn (1833–1912). He was an allegedly mean millionaire businessman of modest origins who, having no natural heirs, left his money for charitable purposes, some of it for endowments he specified, the rest to be allocated by his trustees to humanitarian purposes, including the alleviation of human suffering and the promotion of education. His trustees, having consulted the president of the Royal Society and the secretary of the Medical Research Committee, both Cambridge men, endowed not only the Department of Biochemistry at Cambridge, but also the Dunn Nutritional Laboratory at Cambridge, as well as the Department of Pathology at Oxford, to which they gave £100,000. Between them the Oxford and Cambridge departments have yielded ten Nobel Prize winners, including Hopkins for the discovery of vitamins, and professors Florey and Chain for their developmental work on penicillin. The advisers, to whom one must surely raise one's hat, were Sir William Bate Hardy of Caius College and Sir Walter Morley Fletcher of Trinity.

Fund-Raising in Perspective

A partial indication of how the scale of gifts has varied since 1850 is to be found in Table 4.5. This shows how much of the university's trust income today derives from gifts made in successive decades since 1851, and from gifts made before 1850. The figures measure how much the university benefits today from all the trusts with which it has been endowed that can be dated unambiguously. Two qualifications are necessary.

First, since the earlier gifts often consisted of particular properties that may have appreciated at different rates one from another, the figures for gifts made in the earlier years may not closely represent the value of the initial donations. From the late nineteenth century onwards this qualification fades away; since 1958 the capital of the trusts has been invested in a common fund (on which more in Chapter 7).

Second, the figures do not include the large amount of money that was raised for and invested in buildings and their equipment; nor do they include money given for current expenditure. The latter has been important since fund-raising was revived in the 1980s.

The figures are volatile, but one can see that they rose after 1900 and continued upwards until about 1960, and then dipped. Since the 1980s they have risen sharply.

Fund-raising by the CUA died away after the early 1920s. A suggestion that the association should be reconstituted for the sake of renewed fund-raising was turned down in 1938, and in 1953 it was decided that while no action should be taken formally to wind up the association, the dormant accounts

Table 4.5. The origins of today's trust income

Trusts created in	Income today £
Pre-1850	286,000
1851–60	92,000
1861–70	51,000
1871–80	97,000
1881–90	220,000*
1891–1900	9,000
1901–10	646,000
1911–20	853,000
1921–30	1,409,000
1931–40	884,000
1941–50	2,026,000
1951–60	2,300,000
1961–70	392,000
1971–80	1,074,000
1981–90	1,538,000
1991–2000	3,471,000
2001–10	7,575,000

*Of this figure, £126,000 is the income of three trusts endowed by John Stewart of Rannoch, about whom little is known.

of the CUA should be handed over by the university.[5] Nevertheless there was still a considerable inflow of endowments between 1941 and 1960. Gifts from industry, sometimes solicited by a department, were important. But after this post-war surge the flow died away. The provision of government money came to be taken for granted and charitable giving was held in relatively low esteem. The revival of fund-raising since the 1980s is analysed in Chapter 8.

---

5 History of the Cambridge University Association (Cambridge University Archives, C/S 18.iv.49); and Council Minute 322 of 23 February 1953.

Chapter 5

THE ACQUISITION OF LAND FOR EXPANSION

The university, which now owns a valuable land bank, began in the second half of the nineteenth century to acquire land on which to place buildings for the sciences and other new subjects. Its main purchases from then to today are listed in Table 5.1.

For a long time, building, financed by new endowments and later by government funding, was largely concentrated on the New Museums Site and Downing Site, the two sites which, peppered with buildings mostly for the physical sciences, can be seen today on either side of Pembroke Street and Downing Street (a single street which, like others in central Cambridge, changes its name to flatter the college it passes). First in sequence came the New Museums Site. Then at the turn of the twentieth century the university was able fortuitously to buy from Downing College a large area across the street.[1]

The New Museums Site and Downing Site

The New Museums Site was previously the Botanic Garden. In 1762 Dr Richard Walker, vice-master of Trinity, gave the site, then on the edge of town, to the university in trust for use as a botanic garden.[2] In 1831, the site having become too small and unsatisfactory as a botanic garden, and the university's need for new buildings having become urgent, the university acquired from Trinity Hall 38 acres between Trumpington Road and Hills Road as a new home for the Botanic Garden, in exchange for 7 acres of adjacent land (on which Bateman Street and Norwich Street now stand) and

1 For plans of the Museum and Downing sites in 1865, 1922 and 1950, see: J. P. R. Roach (ed.), *A History of the County of Cambridge and the Isle of Ely* (1959), III: 274; see also Nikolaus Pevsner, *The Buildings of England – Cambridgeshire* (1970), 205 and passim.
2 Robert Willis and J. W. Clark, *The Architectural History of the University of Cambridge* (1886), III: 145; and J. W. Clark, *Endowments of the University of Cambridge* (1904), 468–74.

Table 5.1. Major purchases of Cambridge land by the university

		Purchase		Price per acre
Town land				
1853	Old Botanic Garden	£3,448	for 4 acres	£850
1900 circa	Downing Site: Phase 1 (*on street*)	£15,000	for 2 acres	£7,500
	Phase 2	£2,000	for 0.4 acres	£5,000
	Phase 3	£25,000	for 6.25 acres	£4,000
1920	Scroope House	£14,900	for 3.4 acres	£4,400
1925	New University Library	£12,483	for 7.8 acres	£1,600
1927	Lensfield House	£12,000	for 2.8 acres	£4,300
1948	Sidgwick Avenue Site	£25,000	for 7 acres	£3,571
Total		£109,831	for 33.65 acres	£3,263
Agricultural land west of Cambridge				
1923	from Trinity College	£22,500	for 402 acres	£56
1931	from Prof. H. F. Newall	£3,000	for 32 acres	£94
1947	from St Catherine's College	£11,000	for 54 acres	£203
1948	Madingley Estate	£50,000	for 1,200 acres	£42
1949	from St John's College	£1,024	for 17 acres	£60
1949	from Merton College, Oxford	£10,000	for 100 acres	£100
1949	from Storey's Charity	£1,518	for 20 acres	£76
1998	from Cambridge Perfusion (once Trinity land)	£425,000	for 395 acres	£1,075
Total		£524,000	for 2,220 acres	£236

Note: The table lists the main purchases I have traced. It omits a few purchases west of Cambridge, and some elsewhere.

£2,210.[3] When the removal of the garden was completed in 1853, soon after the introduction of the natural sciences tripos in 1848, the university bought the old site from the Botanic Garden's trustees for £3,448 and appointed a syndicate to consider what new accommodation should be provided on the site. In its report, dated 31 December 1853, the syndicate divided professors into two classes: 'scientific professors' who need museums, laboratories or apparatus rooms as well as a lecture room; and 'literary professors' who need only a lecture room. They proposed one big lecture room for the common use of the literary professors, and a combination of different types of room – museums, laboratories and lecture rooms – for each of the scientific professors according to the requirements of his subject.[4] It was a grand

---

3 C. Crawley, *Trinity Hall: the History of a Cambridge College, 1350–1975* (1976), 121.

4 The report is reproduced verbatim in Willis and Clark, *The Architectural History of the University of Cambridge*, III: 159–65.

scheme. For its implementation a design was commissioned from Anthony Salvin, the leading Gothic revival architect (he designed Whewell's Court for Trinity), but shortage of money meant that his design for the Museum Site was not built as a piece.

As space ran out, the university added to the site by the purchase of two contiguous properties, increasing the area to just over 5 acres. In 1894 it bought, with a gift from two brothers Hopkinson, the old Perse School, after which Free School Lane is named and in the hall of which the Whipple Museum is now housed; and in 1896 it purchased the garden and grounds of Mortlock's bank, which in that year was merged with Barclays to become the bank that until recently stood on Bene't Street. Mr John Mortlock (1755–1816), the founder of the bank, was an eighteenth-century thruster who gained local power and popularity by shameless corruption, yet succeeded as a banker.[5] How different from those Quakers – the Barclays, Lloyds, Gurneys, Peckovers and others – who gained trust as bankers by their austere and honest ways. The wording of a plaque by the entrance to the bank today is remarkable:

John Mortlock
1755–1816
'Master of the Town of Cambridge'

This site was once his home where he opened
the first banking house in
Cambridge

Draper, Banker, MP, Recorder and thirteen times Mayor

'That which you call corruption I call influence'

The Downing Site used to be part of a property of 30 acres of fields and a few dwellings that the master and the first fellows of Downing College bought in 1807 on which to establish their new college.[6] The bequest of the founder, Sir George Downing, had been so much reduced in value by years of legal wrangling over his will – a case that makes Dickens's story of Jarndyce and Jarndyce seem unexaggerated – that the college was able to build and recruit fellows only slowly, and at the end of the century it was ill-placed, because of the poor quality as well as poor quantity of its land, to withstand the effects of the agricultural depression. In the words of the college bursar of the time,

---

5 John D. Pickles, 'John Mortlock, 1755–1816', www.oxforddnb.com.
6 Stanley French, *The History of Downing College, Cambridge* (1978), 85–6.

'every farming tenant of the college went bankrupt or committed suicide, or did both'.[7] Driven to raise money by selling land that was still worth something, the college between 1895 and 1901 sold to the university a strip of land along Downing Street and two parcels of land further into the college grounds. To do so, it sacrificed its entrance on Downing Street and an avenue of limes leading to the college buildings in which nightingales used to sing. Instead it adopted the poky entrance on Regent Street that it uses today. The university paid £15,000 for the first two acres, £5,000 for the next parcel of land and then about £25,000 for the last 6¼ acres.[8]

There can be no question, at least in the case of the third parcel of land, that Downing made a forced sale and the university seized an opportunity to invest in land for future use, not to meet immediate needs. In early 1902 the vice-chancellor, in a letter to the chancellor stating the case for more fund-raising by the Cambridge University Association, wrote:

The one open site remaining in the centre of Cambridge consists of the portion of the Downing College Estate lying between the College precincts and the land already purchased by the University... The authorities of Downing College having recently found themselves compelled to take further steps for the utilisation of their property, it seemed to the Council of the Senate unwise to let so wholly exceptional an opportunity pass of securing a site eminently desirable in itself, and immediately adjacent to that on which University Laboratories and Museums are already being erected. Negotiations were accordingly opened by the Financial Board with the college for the purchase of the whole area in question, amounting to 6 ¼ acres... the terms of an agreement have been provisionally settled. This agreement will shortly be submitted to the Senate for its approval.[9]

The Downing Site was gradually filled with a hotchpotch of buildings to house a great variety of subjects: law, archaeology, ethnology, geology, botany, agriculture, mineralogy, physiology, biochemistry, anatomy, pathology and low temperature research.

In the 1920s, as the Downing Site was filling up, the university bought two houses with large gardens not far away. To meet the needs of the Engineering

---

7 French, *The History of Downing College*, 134.
8 French, *The History of Downing College*, 132; and *Cambridge University Reporter* (1901–2), 225–9, 726–9 and 917.
9 Letter from A. W. Ward, vice-chancellor, to His Grace the Duke of Devonshire, chancellor of the University of Cambridge, 24 March 1902.

School, in 1920 it bought Scroope House, standing in a garden of over 3 acres off Trumpington Street, from Gonville and Caius College, for which it paid £14,900.[10] In 1927 it bought from the executors of Dr Laurence Humphry, an honorary physician at Addenbrooke's, a house called Lensfield with 2.8 acres of grounds for £12,000; and from Downing College it bought a narrow strip of land adjacent to Lensfield. The resulting site stretched along Lensfield Road from the Catholic Church to Panton Street and, in parts, as far back as Union Road.[11] This site was apparently bought with an eye to the future. Temporarily the existing house was put to various uses. The first new building to be erected on the site was the Scott Polar Institute, designed by Sir Herbert Baker (the co-architect with Lutyens of New Delhi), which was completed in 1934, having been paid for by a building fund of £12,000 that had been raised outside the university in memory of Captain Scott.[12] The first part of the new chemistry complex, which now occupies most of the site, was opened in 1956.

It is surprising that at the turn of the twentieth century two houses with such large gardens stood in that area. One might have expected to find housing of greater density so near the centre of Cambridge. But that was then the southern edge of town. Immediately to the south of Scroope House, the Leys School was founded in 1875 'on a leafy 50 acre site'.[13]

The Pitt Building

On the death in 1806 of William Pitt the younger, who had been an undergraduate at Pembroke, a committee was formed in Cambridge to raise money for a statue of him to be placed in the Senate House.[14] When the appeal was heavily oversubscribed – more than £7,500 was received – the surplus was partly returned to subscribers, partly used in 1813 to create the Pitt classical scholarship. But that was not all. In London another appeal for a statue of Pitt was oversubscribed, and the surplus was directed to Cambridge: in 1813 the university was given £500 to augment the endowment of the Pitt scholarship; then in June 1824 the chairman of the London committee,

---

10 T. J. N. Hilken, *Engineering at Cambridge University, 1783–1965* (1967), 155.

11 *Cambridge University Reporter*, 15 June 1926, 1151–2.

12 Cambridge University Association (CUA) Min. IV 4, and *Cambridge University Reporter*, 16 February 1932, 644–5.

13 www.theleys.net/about-us.

14 Willis and Clark, *The Architectural History of the University of Cambridge*, III: 60 and 136–44; and Clark, *Endowments of the University of Cambridge*, 307–9; Pevsner, *The Buildings of England – Cambridgeshire*, passim.

Lord Camden, the chancellor of the university, wrote to the vice-chancellor to say that a meeting of subscribers had unanimously resolved

> that the surplus of the Fund, after defraying the Expense of the Statue in Hanover Square…be applied to the Erection of a Handsome and Appropriate Building at Cambridge, connected with the University Press; such building to bear the name of Mr. Pitt.

This offer was made subject to the condition, put in an earlier letter, that the university should provide a site for erecting the building 'near or opposite Pembroke College'. The university spent nearly £12,000 buying houses that stood on the desired site and nearly £11,000 on the building itself. It had been expected that £9,000 would come from London, but less came because the cost of the London statue, which can be seen in Hanover Square, was more than expected.

Lord Camden on behalf of the London subscribers wrote that 'it will be a most flattering addition to the character and reputation of Mr Pitt that his name should be connected with that Press from which emanate works of enlightened Literature and profound Science'. The press has now moved on to other premises but the building, which was opened by Lord Camden in 1833, still stands.

Building for the Arts

Before 1939 buildings for the arts were not altogether neglected. The university acquired sites near the centre of the town for the Divinity School and for lecture rooms for the arts, and it reached across the river to acquire land for the new university library.

For the Divinity School the university in the 1870s purchased a site from St John's opposite the main entrance to that college. The project was promoted and half paid for by William Selwyn, holder of the Lady Margaret Professorship of Divinity, the most richly endowed chair in the university.[15] (Selwyn College was named after his younger brother, Bishop George Augustus Selwyn.) The university paid St John's £3,790 for the site and directed that, in addition to rooms for divinity, the building should contain lecture rooms for 'literary professors'. The building, in spectacular High Tudor style, was finished in 1879. In the final accounts the cost of the Divinity School is put at £11,060, and the cost of the 'Literary wing' at £4,014. Previously there stood on the site a bakery, stables and dwelling

---

15 See Appendix 1B.

houses, known as the Pentionary of St John's, meaning a place to house fee-paying pensioners.

On Mill Lane the university bought a site in the 1920s from Mr W. Sindall, a builder, on which it in 1925 erected a building for the Board of Extra-Mural Studies (the building in neo-William-and-Mary style that stands back from the street), and in the early 1930s the Mill Lane Lecture Rooms were built for the arts faculties.[16] In 1888 the Local Examinations Syndicate had bought with its own money a site on Mill Lane and built on it.[17]

Expansion to the West

With land for new buildings within the university's traditional bounds exhausted – or available only at exorbitant cost – the university began in the inter-war period to expand westwards. To get land for its planned new library the university in 1922 considered two possible sites beyond the Backs, each of approximately 7 acres.[18] The first was the garden and cricket ground of Corpus Christi College, now the university's Sidgwick Avenue Site. Since Corpus asked £25,000 (about £3,500 an acre), an unrealistically high price, its offer was rejected.[19] Thirty-six years later the university in 1948 paid Corpus precisely that price, but in money devalued by inflation, when it bought the site for the arts faculties.

The alternative site, on which the library now stands, was a cricket field belonging jointly to Clare and King's, which the two colleges agreed in 1922 to sell to the university for £1,600 an acre, a low price compared with what was paid for comparable sites at that time (Table 5.1). The Financial Board accepted the offer and minuted,

> That the Financial Board records its appreciation of the governing bodies of Clare College and King's College in so readily assisting the University to provide a suitable site for the new University Library.[20]

It is understandable that Clare and King's were willing sellers. Their cricket field had been requisitioned in 1914 as the site for a temporary military

---

16 CUA Min. II 10, 20 May 1931.

17 CUA Min. II 2, 10 March 1885.

18 In what follows, I have drawn freely on Philomena Guillebaud's excellent detailed histories of the development of west Cambridge since enclosure in *Proceedings of the Cambridge Antiquarian Society* (*PCAS*) 96, 97 and 98. I am greatly indebted to her.

19 CUA Min. II 8, letter of 24 January 1922 from Charles Pollock, master of Corpus Christi College to the secretary of the Financial Board.

20 CUA Min. II 8, 71; and *Cambridge University Reporter*, 23 May 1922, 978–80.

hospital of 1,200 beds in 24 huts. To the dismay of the two colleges, the huts were taken over at the end of the war by the local government and converted at considerable cost to use as emergency housing.[21] King's and Clare tried to get the land back, but by 1921 they were so uncertain when, if ever, they would succeed, that they bought land on Barton Road and established an alternative cricket ground. Before the local authorities agreed to give up the land many letters passed between the two colleges, their lawyers, their land agents, and several government agencies.[22] The sale to the university was completed in November 1925 when £12,483 was paid for the site.[23]

Most of the land further to the west that the university and colleges have acquired has come from two owners, St John's College and the Madingley Estate.

From its foundation St John's owned a substantial area of land beyond the Backs, which from the late nineteenth century onwards it sold for middle-class housing, notably on Grange Road and the newly built roads off it, and for academic use;[24] 'there was clearly an unwritten consensus among the college landowners that residential development in west Cambridge was to be restricted to a relatively affluent market and strictly controlled to avoid deterioration in property values.'[25] Associated with this approach was the sentiment amongst the great and the good of Cambridge that an unspoilt hinterland should be preserved to the west of the Backs where, beyond an area of big houses, gardens and playing fields, the Coton footpath invited the don and his family to escape into a landscape of fields, hedgerows and grazing flocks; a sentiment that was fostered by the admirable Cambridge Preservation Society, founded in 1928, as it raised funds to buy threatened land in this area and other areas, notably the Gogs. For academic use, land was sold by St John's for the University Observatory, for Westminster College, part of Newnham College, Trinity Old Field, Trinity Burrell's Field, Clare Hall, Robinson College, Churchill College, and for part of the West Cambridge Site on which science buildings have recently been developed.

21 Philomena Guillebaud, *PCAS* 97: 181–2; and R. Saundby, 'An open–air military hospital: the First Eastern Military Hospital' *British Medical Journal* 2, 28 November 1914, 942–3.

22 King's College Archives, KCAR/3/1/1/8/31 and 32.

23 Financial Board minutes of 14 July 1925, CUA Min. II 8; and King's College Archives, KCAR/7/GAR/11, 17 November 1925.

24 J. S. Boys Smith, *Memories of St John's College, Cambridge, 1919–1969* (1983), 162–3, 184–92.

25 Philomena Guillebaud, *PCAS* 96: 199.

The Madingley Estate

The manorial estate of Madingley of nearly 3,000 acres to the west of Cambridge was split in two in 1859 after its owner, 'an overenthusiastic sportsman and gambler', was obliged by his debts to transfer the estate to his two sisters.[26] In 1903 Trinity bought one half of the estate, paying £41,250 for 1,413 acres.[27] In two large purchases and several small ones the university subsequently bought more than half this Trinity land. In 1923 it persuaded the college to sell it 402 acres for £22,500 to serve as an enlarged farm for the use of the School of Agriculture, the creation of which was described in Chapter 3. The land it then bought, which lies between Madingley Road and Huntingdon Road, consisted of Howe Hill Farm and most of Gravel Hill Farm (which the university had rented from Trinity since 1910), less the frontage along the Huntingdon Road, running approximately from Storeys Way to today's motorway, which the college sold for the ribbon development of housing that is visible today.[28] The second purchase was in 1998 when the university bought Catch Hall Farm, comprising 395 acres of Madingley land that Trinity had sold in 1945 to Messrs Chivers and Sons, a farming company, as part of its policy of disposing of poor agricultural land. The land had since changed hands. The university paid more than £1,000 an acre for it, an increase in the price of land in that area since 1949 that matches the rise in the general price level in that period.[29]

When the other half of the Madingley Estate (reduced by some sales of land to 1,200 acres) came on the market in 1948, the university bought it for £50,000.[30] Whereas the part bought by Trinity consisted of farms, this half included Madingley Hall and the village. The university's main interest in its acquisition was the possible use of the hall and its outbuildings as a residential college or for use by the Board of Extra-Mural Studies, but the council of the Senate decided that all 1,200 acres should be bought. This was opposed by Tressillian Nicholas, the senior bursar of Trinity and a member of the university's Estates Committee, who argued that the land was so poor that the

---

26 A. P. M. Wright and C. P. Lewis (eds), *The Victorian History of the Counties of England: Cambridge and the Isle of Ely* (1989), IX: 179–82; and minutes of the Financial Board, 14 January 1948, CUA Min. II 16.

27 Trinity College accounts, 1902–3; and Trinity College Council minutes of 10, 24, and 31 October and 14 November 1902.

28 Trinity College accounts, 1922–3, and *Cambridge University Reporter*, 6 February 1923, 620–1.

29 Consumer prices, as measured by the Office for National Statistics series CDKO, rose 20 times between 1949 and 1998; so roughly did the price of land shown in Table 5.1 above.

30 Minutes of the Financial Board, 14 January 1948, CUA Min. II 16.

estate should be bought only on the condition that those parts of it that were not needed for university purposes should be sold 'in the near or fairly near future'. His advice was not heeded: in 1950 the council decided that no part of the estate should be sold. The university's holdings of Madingley land were thus increased to approximately 2,000 acres.

In this case Nicholas was no doubt applying his sharp geologist's eye for the quality of land. After he became bursar of Trinity in 1929 he persuaded Trinity that, when possible, it should sell poor agricultural land, which comprised a substantial part of its initial endowment by Henry VIII, and put the proceeds into shop property and into 'good permanent grassland and highly fertile silt land'.[31] In pursuit of the latter policy the college in 1933 bought the Trimley Estate of nearly 4,000 acres on the Suffolk coast. On it, quite unforeseen by him or anyone else, now stands the Felixstowe Dock, bringing millions in rent to Trinity. Investment is a chancy business.[32]

The university paid for its Madingley purchase by using a bequest worth £28,000 and by taking a temporary advance from the emergency fund that had been set aside during the war to meet arrears of maintenance. The bequest was that of Mr Henry Finnis Blosse Lynch (1862–1913) of Trinity, a businessman, traveller in the Middle East, and politician who left half his estate, subject to a life interest in favour of his sister, to the university entirely free of conditions, adding the words 'which is the best contribution I think I can make to the public objects of the present day'. With the death of his sister the money came to the university in 1948.[33]

Post-war Policy and Purchases

After the 1939–45 war the university began actively to consider acquiring land for future development, probably prompted not just by the expectation that it would need more land in the new era of university expansion, but also by the knowledge that the UGC might provide non-recurrent grants for land purchases as well as for other capital expenditure. A paper prepared for the UGC in October 1946 reported that 'where to expand is under discussion with the local authorities'.[34] Shortly afterwards a Sites Committee was created

---

31 Report of the senior bursar to the Trinity College Finance Committee, 19 January 1945, item 3.

32 Robert Neild, *Riches and Responsibility: the Financial History of Trinity College* (2008), 100–104.

33 Christopher N. B. Ross, 'Lynch, Henry Finnis Blosse (1862–1913)' www.oxforddnb. com; and *Cambridge University Reporter*, 4 May 1915, 838–9, and 18 May 1948, 1172.

34 Paper prepared for a visitation by the UGC attached to minutes of the Financial Board meeting of 16 October 1946, CUA Min. II 16.

to advise on the 'long-term planning of sites belonging to the University and advise on which sites the University might acquire';[35] and in 1947 Laundry Farm of 54 acres on Barton Road was bought for £11,000 from St Catharine's College with the help of a grant from the UGC. A letter sent by the treasurer of the university to the bursar of the college in July 1946 said:

> The immediate problem is to meet the needs of developments in nuclear physics and allied sciences, but the Council have in mind the desirability of securing a site of sufficient size to provide space for the University's probable needs for many years to come.[36]

Subsequently, planning permission having been refused, the farm was not developed (it is now used as a depot by the university's maintenance branch). The university then turned its attention to other land on the west of Cambridge and put together the West Cambridge Site, mostly by buying land in 1949. The main purchases are listed in Table 5.1. The largest was from Merton College, Oxford, whose founder, Walter de Merton, besides founding early in the thirteenth century the Oxford college that bears his name, also bought land in Cambridge for reasons that are unclear.

It was a considerable time before the university through its ponderous democratic procedures agreed that any department should be moved from its heartland in the town to this western hinterland. In 1958, the Senate approved a 'Report of the Council on the provision and development of sites for University use'.[37] Just over two pages long, it recommended that the university's needs should be met by redeveloping existing central sites, including the erection of 'one or two buildings of more than seven stories' in the centre of the Museum Site so as to increase its capacity 'by as much as a third', and by 'the acquisition of further central sites as opportunity may offer'. The report acknowledged that 'it may not ultimately be practicable or desirable for all University work to be carried out on central sites', but it did not look ahead.

The tide was turned in 1965 by a report of 69 pages, including appendices, that was produced by a committee of four distinguished scientists, all Fellows of the Royal Society, chaired by W. A. Deer, geologist and master of Trinity Hall. The others were E. C. Bullard, J. B. Hutchinson, and J. C. Kendrew. Having held 30 formal meetings during which they assembled statistics and

---

35 CUA Min. II 16, 6 November 1946 and 21 November 1946.
36 St Catharine's College Archives, file EST/BAR/5/1.
37 'Report of the Council of the Senate on the provision and development of sites for University use', *Cambridge University Reporter*, 26 November 1958, 432–4.

interviewed heads of departments and others, they offered much information about trends in the number of students, teachers and assistant staff, as well as information, with maps, about the evolution of the university's various sites; and about the subjects within the sciences that were likely to expand. (They rightly predicted the expansion of biology.) They proposed that the university should keep a rolling plan with short-, medium- and long-term horizons. Their most important recommendation was that a new science site in west Cambridge, which had been proposed before, should now be developed, and that physics should urgently be moved there.[38] The New Cavendish Laboratory was completed on the site in 1974.

Development on an important scale is now underway, or at an advanced stage of planning, on two parts of the university's west Cambridge estate: the West Cambridge Site, on which building has been proceeding apace; and the North West Cambridge Site.

The West Cambridge Site

The West Cambridge Site is a dented rectangle of land of some 170 acres that lies between the Madingley Road to the north and the Coton Footpath to south, and between Clerk Maxwell Road and the M11 to the east and west.

In 1955 the Veterinary School, previously on Milton Road, was moved to the site, initially making use of the adjacent fields. After that there was a lull till the early 1970s when the Cavendish Laboratory was moved to the site, and the Whittle Laboratory and Schofield Centre were built, one containing jet engines and the other a large centrifuge, both unsuited to a site in the town. Since then a number of new university laboratories have been established there, principally in the rapidly evolving physical sciences. Recent additions have been nanoscience and the physics of medicine. Also on the site are three science-based private firms – Schlumberger, Microsoft and Aveva; and some blocks of flats that have been built by the university for leasing to newly appointed staff. Since the buildings mostly are low and surrounded by large parking areas, the density of building is low. The contrast with the overcrowded New Museum and Downing sites is extreme. It is like the difference between Manhattan and a shopping centre on the outskirts of a provincial American town. As regards aesthetics, almost any development of land to the west of Cambridge will be in some degree at odds with the aims of the Cambridge Preservation Society, but nothing

---

38 'Report to the General Board of the Committee of the Board on the Long term Needs of Scientific Departments', *Cambridge University Reporter*, 8 December 1965, paras 95 and 113.

could be more discordant with those aims, or more offensive in appearance to any sensitive person, than the West Cambridge Site today; nor, I gather, do the occupants of the bleak blocks of laboratories and flats much like their surroundings.

The North West Cambridge Site

The North West Cambridge Site of 225 acres forms a triangle between Madingley Road, Huntingdon Road and the M11. It is part of the land that was sold to the university by Trinity in 1923 to serve as the enlarged university farm, and it is still part of that farm. A consultative 'green paper' describing the project was circulated for comment in June 2010.[39] It seems that the principal aim of the project is to provide urgently needed affordable housing for university staff. To help finance this, it is proposed that a considerable part of the land should be sold to developers for private housing. It is planned that 3,000 housing units should be created, 'half of which would be for renting to University staff, with the balance for sale in the open market'. There would also be good infrastructure, a primary school, community facilities, a hotel and green spaces, and land would be provided for commercial firms as well as university departments to undertake research.[40] What is envisaged seems to be a venture in which permission is obtained to sell a considerable area for private housing, thereby raising money with which to build housing for academics and students, and some academic and commercial facilities for research: a new suburb of Cambridge would be created that would help to house its swelling population. The proportion of the 225 acres allocated to academic activity is small – some part of the 16 per cent labelled 'Academic and commercial research':

	%
Housing	57
Academic and commercial research	16
Student housing	5
Hotel/conference facility	2
Local centre (including primary school)	4
Open space	9
Roads	6
Other	1

---

39 'North West Cambridge Project: A Green Paper', *Cambridge University Reporter* 6194, 25 June 2010, para. 25.
40 Ibid. paras 26 and 43.

The University Farm

The Cambridge School of Agriculture was closed in the 1960s after social change and the upgrading of the pass-degree course in agriculture to an honours course had led to a slump in numbers attracted to the school, and the government had decided that fewer such schools were needed. Scientists from the school were moved into other departments or went to government research institutions; and its agricultural economists were moved to an expanded Department of Land Economy where, in keeping with the times, the sons of landowners learning to manage their estates gave way to students from all walks being prepared for careers as estate agents and planners.[41]

The university farm, which has always been run, so far as possible, on commercial lines so that teaching should be realistic and the university prudent, has over the years been handed the task of managing the agricultural land that the university has acquired to the west of Cambridge. In all it farms 2,626 acres, of which 1,729 acres, mostly around Madingley, belong to the university; the rest is nearly all rented from colleges.[42] The farm's commercial policy is now distorted for the sake of teaching only to the extent that a herd of cows is kept although the land is not suitable for them, so that students from the Veterinary School may be taught how to handle calving; and some research into potatoes is undertaken, funded from outside the university. Essentially, the farm now serves to look after the university's investment in land to the west of Cambridge.

Conclusion

Between 1923 and 1953 the university by design and accident acquired a major landbank to the west of Cambridge at an average price of £54 an acre, a figure which looks astonishingly low today. Since then the growth in the demand for land, combined with the tight restriction of the supply by planning law, has caused the price of land to soar wherever there is a prospect that development may be permitted. Recently agricultural land adjacent to the New Addenbrooke's site on the outskirts of Cambridge was sold to a medical research organisation for nearly £2 million an acre.

---

41 For the official account of these events, see the *Cambridge University Reporter*, 1 November 1967, 517–33, and 31 January 1968, 1134–6. For a lively and highly personal account of the political manoeuvring over the reallocation of department's resources, see D. R. Denman, *A Half and Half Affair, Chronicles of a Hybrid Don* (1993) 190–1.

42 'Cambridge University Farm', an admirable pamphlet by Dr Jeff Jones, manager of the university farm.

The university's land to the west does not have immediate value of anything like that magnitude. Its planning designation is for educational use only. But the North West Cambridge project is a case where it is expected that private development of housing will be permitted, so as to help finance the development of university housing and other university facilities on the site: development value will be realised. Nobody knows how the economy and planning law will change in the centuries ahead, but so long as the economy and population grow, increasing demand for land will generate pressure for land to be released for development. On the other hand, one hopes that the aim of preserving green fields in this area will not be neglected by the university. The university has an asset that has been and will continue to be well worth cherishing for both financial and aesthetic reasons.

There are other benefits to consider too. Since the university has owned land designated for educational use it has not had to go into the market to buy land at high prices, and that should continue to be the case. Further, since the transactions in land amongst the colleges and the university described in this chapter took place at a time of low prices, they have not entailed, as high prices would have done, large transfers of wealth between one member and another of the academic family.

Chapter 6

THE *ANCIEN RÉGIME*

After the 1939–45 war the financial circumstances of the university were transformed in three ways:

1. Governments of all parties adopted the policy of providing free higher education.
2. In place of economic depression there was full employment, economic growth and inflation.
3. Competition amongst nations and firms to develop new products, military and civil, led to a great increase in public and private spending on scientific research.

The last two changes require no explanation. To appreciate the first, one must recall what went before.

Before the 1939–45 war money was what bought entry to Oxford or Cambridge colleges for most students. All that a boy who was not of scholarship calibre required in order to be accepted as an undergraduate was that his family had enough money to pay his way, that he had imbibed a modicum of education at school, and that his schoolmaster (usually a housemaster since most came from private schools) recommended him to a college, preferably one with which that master, the candidate's family, or both, had connections. At the women's colleges, of which there were only two, competition for places was more intense than at the men's colleges. They had fewer endowed scholarships than the average men's college, but they benefited more from Fisher's state scholarships, since the fraction given to women – one half – was high in relation to the number of women going to British universities at that time.[1]

From their early days the colleges had consisted of fellows and scholars financed from endowment income, plus fee-paying students, known as pensioners, the number of which grew erratically over the centuries.

---

1 See Chapter 3.

After slumping in the eighteenth century when Cambridge was at its most decadent and smart young men went on the Grand Tour, the number of pensioners increased rapidly in the nineteenth and twentieth centuries, while the number of scholars increased little. The colleges became institutions that combined an endowed component of fellows and scholars with an ever-larger component of fee-paying students. Dennis Robertson, the economist, likened Trinity in 1938 to a combination of a monastery and a boarding school, and explored whether the boarding school was subsidising the monastery.[2]

Many of the fee-paying students were poll-men (or pass-men) who typically sought amusement, not learning, and were notorious for their idleness and frivolity. They were admitted to study for an 'ordinary degree' (also known as a poll or pass degree) for which they were examined on subject matter little different from that which they should have learnt at school. Many of them did not bother to take exams since they did not care whether they gained a degree; many failed.

When reform of the university got under way in the middle of the nineteenth century, it was proposed that action be taken to get rid of idle poll-men, but they lived on in substantial numbers till after the 1939–45 war.

The Debate over Poll-Men

Some printed flysheets circulated in the 1860s give a taste of the debate. Mr Joseph Bickersteth Mayor of St John's, a stern reformer, wrote:

> Let us exact a higher standard in the schools [meaning the departments of the university], let us no longer brand a Poll man a 'non-reading' man; above all let persons in authority cease to wink at and openly encourage idleness and expensive habits, as signs of high breeding and good fortune, and we shall soon rid the University and Colleges of the stigma, that it is not the man but the fees which form the object of their solicitude...
>
> I think we are bound to make men work, or to get rid of them; and I have no fear that our numbers would ultimately be lessened by doing so. As a rule, I think no man should do less than five hours' reading in the day...[3]

---

2 Robert Neild, *Riches and Responsibility: the Financial History of Trinity College, Cambridge* (2008), 158–9.

3 Joseph Bickersteth Mayor, 'Considerations upon the Poll Course addressed to the Members of the Senate of the University of Cambridge', Trinity College Library, LL 696 c 118, 7.

To achieve these aims Mayor proposed that the poll examination be somewhat revised: that Greek be removed from the classics component on the grounds that too little was demanded to be worthwhile; similarly that mechanics and hydrostatics be removed from the maths; and that the place of the modern arts subjects be increased by expanding the history component and adding geography. He further advocated the introduction of a matriculation exam. But, rather than making the passing of the exam a condition of entry to the university, he proposed that it could be taken during the first year, so that '...a man need not be deprived of the benefit of college residence because he had failed to pass in the first examination. The University might refuse to allow any term before that in which he passed, but that would not necessitate his being sent down from the College.'[4] Mr Girdlestone of Christ's supported him but disagreed with him on details.[5]

On the other side of the debate was Leslie Stephen. He held that 'it is simply impossible to "make men work".'[6] To attempt to do so would reduce the number admitted to the university and would not induce a compensating rise in the state of education elsewhere.

Before saying what should be done, he posed the question: 'What is the aim which the university should keep chiefly in view?' The answer, he said, 'is easily given':

> Our aim should be, as I believe Mr Mayor will agree with me in thinking, to exercise the strongest influence we can in raising the general tone of instruction amongst the highly educated classes...[7]
>
> What parents and their sons seek for here, when they do not seek for fellowships or higher honours is the moral and social training, and not the few scraps of learning which we throw at them. I do not ask just now if this is right or wrong. I say that it is the fact, and that if every one of Mr Mayor's proposed reforms were carried out tomorrow, it would still be the fact, that the intellectual element of the Poll-man's education is merely trifling, and that the moral and social element is altogether predominant. My opinion of the common sense of my countrymen would be considerably lower if I thought otherwise. I can see that a young man of slight education may gain a great deal by mixing with society here.

---

4 Mayor, 'Considerations upon the Poll Course', 11.
5 W. H. Girdlestone, 'The Poll Course Considered from Another Point of View' (1862), Trinity College Library, LL 696 c 118, passim.
6 Leslie Stephen, 'The Poll Degree from a Third Point of View' (1863), Trinity College Library, LL 696 c 118, 5.
7 Leslie Stephen, 'The Poll Degree', 8–9.

I can see that he is benefited morally by constant intercourse with the most high-spirited and ablest young men of his own age, whether in cricket-clubs, boat-clubs, or any other kind of club. I can see that the various traditions of the University, the healthy and manly life to which most of our students are accustomed, form a good and even noble training for a young man. It is in fact one of the most characteristic growths of English society, and I hope it may long flourish. But if any one tells me that the benefits which the University confers upon such a man are that it teaches him in three years to stumble through a bit of Virgil or do a Rule of Three sum, I can only reply that my ideas of education are very different from his.[8]

Leslie Stephens's solution was to apply 'the ordinary principles of supply and demand' to the granting of degrees. Improvement should be sought not by keeping candidates out but by increasing the attractiveness and value of the education offered. This he would achieve by abolishing altogether the Poll Examination and adding to the existing triposes new papers in subjects that would be accessible to the former poll-man. Thus he proposed that moral sciences tripos have added to it papers in some definite periods of history, in some simpler parts of political economy and, perhaps, in some given book of jurisprudence.

In hindsight, this debate is remarkable for its insularity. Since the French Revolution, the governments of France, Germany and other countries had taken to subsidising scientific education in order to increase their military and economic strength. The seminal innovation had been the creation of the École Polytechnique by the French revolutionary government in 1794 with the task of training students, for whom all costs were paid, in maths and the physical sciences in order to prepare them for service of the state. It was the model that was followed in the creation of Technische Hochschulen in other European countries in the mid-nineteenth century; in the United States it was the model for MIT, which was created as a private institution in 1861. Yet here we see Cambridge at that very time debating reform on the assumption that

1. apart from scholars, students paid their way and so must come from those classes that had money; no money would come from the state; and
2. fee-paying students were not interested in science or engineering and must be attracted by better courses in the arts. Of the three participants in the debate Leslie Stephen alone mentions the natural

8 Leslie Stephen, 'The Poll Degree', 11.

sciences, but only to say, 'Of the Natural Sciences Tripos I am not qualified to speak'.

The Evidence of the Royal Commission of 1922

The royal commission of 1922 collected statistics of how many poll-men there were at each college at Oxford and Cambridge. Their report showed what percentage of entrants in each year from 1905 to 1909 obtained (a) a pass degree and (b) no degree. The percentages are high at both Oxford and Cambridge, and at both they differ greatly from college to college, and to a lesser extent, from year to year. At Cambridge in 1909: [9]

1. Forty per cent of undergraduates took a pass degree or no degree at 10 out of the 20 colleges. There was much variation between colleges. At most colleges the percentage who took no degree was considerably smaller than that for those who took a pass degree.
2. Outstandingly 'bad' at Cambridge were Trinity Hall, Magdalene, Corpus and Selwyn, each with over 60 per cent taking a pass degree or no degree. 'Good', with low percentages, were King's, Girton and Newnham. King's in reforming itself from its exceptionally bad old ways (by statute it used to admit only Etonians and they received BA degrees without having to take any exam) had not only opened its doors to non-Etonians in 1861 but had decided in 1869 that all Kingsmen must read for an honours degree and must take an entrance exam (if not taking the scholarship exam). In this it leapt ahead of other men's colleges, most of which did not introduce an entrance exam till after the 1939–45 war.[10] At Girton and Newnham there was strong competition for entry, entrance examinations were in place and there was no tradition of frivolous idlers.

The figures for Trinity College, Cambridge and Christ Church, Oxford, those grand sister colleges founded by Henry VIII, are rather high and much alike:

	Percentage who took:	
	A pass degree	No degree
Christ Church 1909	20	27
Trinity, Cambridge 1909	20	25

---

9 *Report of the Royal Commission on Oxford and Cambridge Universities* (1922), 1588, Appendices, 183–5.
10 L. P. Wilkinson, *A Century of King's 1874–1974* (1980), 5–6.

The royal commission welcomed the introduction at Cambridge of the poll course in agriculture for undergraduates destined to own and manage estates, described in Chapter 3:

The new School is very popular, and now contains hundreds of students. More than half their number are landowners, generally intending to farm their own land.[11]

The commissioners, like Leslie Stephen, clearly valued the recruitment of the upper classes and were untroubled by the exam results of the School of Agriculture: of the 321 students enrolled in 1920–21, 50 per cent failed their exam or took none.[12]

The Royal Commission's Conclusions

The commission's general assessment of poll-men, whom they called pass-men, was this:

Objections have been raised in some quarters to the presence of Pass Men in the universities. We submit recommendations in paragraphs 184 to 188 below for imposing a University Entrance Examination (or its equivalent), which will tend to eliminate students of insufficient intellectual calibre, some of whom would no doubt have been Pass Men if admitted to the University. But we are not in favour of the abolition of the Pass degree. Great improvements have recently been made at both Universities in the Pass courses and education, and the Pass students are much more serious than they used to be. Their record in after-life proves on examination to be very good; many of them hold important positions and have become valuable citizens... The abolition of the Pass degree would flood the Honours courses with students for whom a more general education is desirable, and the Honours standards of teaching would suffer. In many men ability of a genuine kind, but not suited to specialisation, requires a more general education than that afforded by an honours course.[13]

---

11 *Report of the Royal Commission* (1922), 37. The author of this passage was probably G. M. Trevelyan, historian, and master of Trinity from 1940 to 1951, who, a member of the commission, is reported to have contributed the passages about Cambridge. A country-loving member of a Northumberland landowning family, he in 1945 rented from the college the shooting over Moor Barns Farm near Madingley when it became available (see the minutes of Trinity College Council, 1 October 1945).

12 *Cambridge University Reporter*, 29 November 1921, 272.

13 *Report of Royal Commission* (1922), 42.

The commission's subsequent discussion of entrance examinations showed the position to be highly unsatisfactory.[14] There was still no university statute requiring the passing of any examination before 'matriculation', the formal ceremony of admission to the university, 'and in fact all students presented by the Colleges for Matriculation are accepted by the University without question, and without any enquiry into their qualifications.' There were college entry exams and also a university exam known as the Previous Examination, but 'there have hitherto been numerous cases in which Colleges have permitted individual entrants to take the examination after admission.'

The commission recommended that

> ...in future the previous passing of a University Entrance Examination should be a rigid condition of entrance to Colleges, Halls and Hostels, and to the Non-Collegiate bodies. In addition, Colleges could continue to impose their own entrance tests so far as they may consider it necessary to do so.

This recommendation was obeyed, but the standard was set so low, and so much discretion was left to the colleges, that students of limited intellectual ability and little ambition continued to be let in. More of them than before may have gone for Honours courses, which now included many new subjects. At Trinity, the only college for which I have statistics, the proportion of poll-men amongst the undergraduates was approximately halved between the wars, but their performance in exams continued to be remarkably poor (Table 6.1).

In the inter-war years, economic pressures told against restriction of admissions. Most families in Britain felt so poor and degrees were so little valued by employers that demand for places was weak. I have heard tell that the junior bursars of small colleges pleaded with the tutors to admit more students so as to fill the rooms and bring in the room rents.

Table 6.1. The performance of poll-men at Trinity, 1909, 1921 and 1938

	1909	1921	1938
Poll-men as % of undergraduates in residence	24	24	13
Failures as % of exams taken			
Poll-men	33	35	26
Honours	13	14	8

Source: Trinity College Archives, Senior Tutors' Reports.

---

14 *Report of Royal Commission* (1922), 166–7.

The Ethos of the *Ancien Régime*

A sharp, rather waggish, portrayal of the *ancien régime* is to be found in a book on Cambridge published in 1940 by a Kingsman who earlier had written about the artistic taste of the Victorians.[15]

> Cambridge and Oxford enjoy a prestige which is not shared by any other universities and is approached perhaps only by Harvard, Yale and Princeton. This is due partly to their antiquity, but that attribute is shared by many universities from Uppsala to Coimbra; it is not due to their standard of learning, which is higher in many other universities. It is due very largely to their expensiveness, for despite scholarships and state-aid, Cambridge and Oxford still remain the homes of privilege, where the man of moderate means has endless advantages over the man of no means at all. It is no good being priggish about this or saying that the earliest colleges were founded for poor scholars; they certainly were, but so, for example, was Harrow. The two universities do not live only on the fact of privilege, nor do they exist only for those who are privileged by birth or income. But they do exist very largely on and for those, and are among the few places now left in the world of Levelling, where inequality is given proper recognition.

He asks, what is Cambridge for? and answers:

> It is for those who want to go there. The reason may be snobbish, and to have such a wish may be a sign of improvidence, but there are parents who feel that their sons can benefit by three years of mixing with other people's sons on terms of friendship governed by conventions of a world that is no longer schoolboy and not yet fully adult...
>
> For three years the undergraduate can do as he likes: he can get drunk or stay sober, read for Honours or take a pass degree; and run through every affectation known even to Kingsmen. He can be as serious or as inconsequent as he likes, though if he persistently flout authority he will be sent down, and if he persistently flout public opinion he will be 'sent up'.[16] But there is at least an even chance that in those years he will acquire a standard of values which may make for happiness and may

---

15 John Steegman, *Cambridge: As it Was and as it is Today* (1940), 103–5. His principal books were *The Rule of Taste from George I to George IV* (1936) and *Victorian Taste: A Study of the Arts and Architecture from 1830 to 1870* (1950).

16 I.e. debagged or thrown into a fountain.

give him a balance between leisure and endeavour in his professional life later on.

The poor man from the elementary school really does not get very much out of Cambridge. He is not likely to make many friends and will almost certainly remain a fish out of water. He would be much wiser to go to one of the newer universities where he would feel less disconnected with his lot...

Nor is it worthwhile for the very rich man, who gets no more out of it than the poor one. There is a rich set at Cambridge, but it is small and limited principally to Trinity, a college so vast that it contains something of everything. The rich man will have a much better time at Oxford, if that is what he wants.

In sum, Cambridge until after the 1939–45 war, like Oxford, was an odd institution: a set of educational charities, mostly created and endowed in a distant religious era, to which a numerically dominant fee-paying population had accrued and which, since the 1914–18 war, had received a regular government subsidy, largely because the government recognised the need to train scientists and the value of the research they did in their university laboratories. In the colleges great and less-great scientists and humanists on High Table co-existed with students below the dais of varied wealth, talents, tastes and behaviour. That Oxford and Cambridge were long considered the 'best places' is not a very significant accolade. Until after the Napoleonic Wars, they were the only universities in England and Wales.

Poll-men and their like were finally squeezed out in the years after the 1939–45 war, when government subsidies for students came in and money no longer bought entry: merit ruled. As a Fabian socialist active in that era, I of course wholly approve of that revolution, and of the later revolution that at last put women on an equal footing with men. But I cannot forget what an often tiresome, but sometimes engaging, breed the poll-men could be. The grander ones might keep a horse and spend their time at the Pitt Club, that local replica of a London club, and at Newmarket. When excited they might let off their spirits by blowing a hunting horn in the courts at night. I chanced to become slightly acquainted with two. First of all, there was Reggie Paget, a passionate horseman who, 50 years after he first rode in the Cottenham point-to-point when a Trinity undergraduate, came back to ride again in the 1970s. Having come off after a few fences, he came hobbling back, chuckling with joy and declaring what a marvellous experience it had been. A radical member of the squirearchy, he had read law for a year, and then military studies for an ordinary degree that he never collected; on the strength of which he became a barrister and a politician of idiosyncratic opinions, renowned for having been simultaneously a Labour MP and master of the Pytchley, one of the grandest packs of foxhounds in the country. His father, having been briefly an independent conservative MP in the 1920s, had died in a hunting accident.[17]

Then, perhaps the last of the breed, there was Patrick Tritton, a man gilded with Irish charm who achieved notoriety when an undergraduate in the mid-1950s for allegedly taking his horse to lectures and, according to another story, for having ridden in Trinity from Nevile's Court to Great Court, up the steps, through the Screens Passage and down the other side. After he left in 1957, having been awarded a 'special' (meaning a specially poor mark) in Part I History and a second in Arabic, he roamed South America on horseback before settling in Mexico. There, married for some years to Nancy Oakes, an extremely rich heiress with a remarkable past, he established a hunt, having bought hounds in Britain and taken them across the Atlantic and down by road through the United States.[18] 'Cambridge', said Walter Ullmann, who taught him history at Trinity, 'is very dull now that merit has taken over and there are no more characters like Tritton'.[19] I encountered Tritton when, in the early summer of 1957, I was woken in my rooms in Trinity's Great Court after the sun was up by the repeated sound below my window of a hunting horn and a man calling to a friend in nearby rooms to come down and have another drink. The porters having persuaded him, at my prompting, to go to bed, I received the next day a most gracious apology. A year or two later, when I chanced to be in Mexico City, he, having heard I was there, took me out for a very jolly evening to make amends.

---

17 Obituary of Major Thomas Guy Frederick Paget, *The Times*, 13 March 1952.
18 Nancy Oakes was daughter of Sir Harry Oakes, the Canadian owner of the richest goldmine in the western hemisphere, whose murder in the Bahamas in 1943 led to a sensational trial in which Nancy's first husband was the prime suspect. Amidst much publicity she gave evidence and he got off. See the obituary of Nancy Oakes von Hoyningen-Huene, *The Times*, 21 January 2005.
19 Obituary of Patrick Tritton, *The Times*, 14 February 1998. An extraordinarily charming and amusing tribute that is well worth looking up.

Chapter 7

GOVERNMENT POLICY SINCE 1945

During the 1939–45 war the coalition government formulated and published plans for post-war social reforms. In the case of education, for which R. A. Butler was minister, legislation was enacted before the war ended. The Education Act of 1944 laid down that the school-leaving age was to be raised in two stages to 16 and the school system reformed. Since these changes were sure to lead to an increased flow of students seeking to enter universities, the UGC in January 1945, before the war was over, represented to the Treasury that much more money would be needed for the universities and proposed an immediate increase in the recurrent grant for the two years 1945 and 1946 to £4.1 million, compared with £2.1 million in 1939, an increase that would more than match inflation.[1] The committee promised to present in two years time a five-year assessment of the universities' needs.

The Golden Age

There followed a golden age for the universities in which they were favoured in an extraordinary degree relative to the rest of the economy and to other types of social expenditure. In spite of the economic hardships of the post-war years, successive chancellors of the exchequer gave the UGC everything it asked for and sometimes more.[2]

In 1945 Sir John Anderson, chancellor of the exchequer in the wartime coalition government, accepted the UGC's submission and set the yearly recurrent grant at £4.1 million for 1945 and 1946, plus £1 million a year for medical education, for which a separate case had been made. Then in March 1947, the Labour chancellor of the exchequer, Hugh Dalton, met the UGC's quinquennial submission by agreeing to a recurrent grant rising from £9 million for 1947–48 to £12 million in 1951–52, and in an open letter to the universities said he was prepared to ask Parliament 'for further increases

1 Robert O. Berdahl, *British Universities and the State* (1959), 70–71.
2 Berdahl, *British Universities*, 70–75.

for well-prepared plans'.[3] In addition, he accepted the UGC's assessment that the universities needed £50 million for capital expenditure, but said that shortage of steel and other supplies would probably limit spending to £20 million. The report of the Barlow committee, one of several assessments of special needs to feed into the UGC submission, had called for the number of scientists and technologists to be doubled in ten years. The physical sciences were now valued as never before.

The austere Sir Stafford Cripps, who succeeded Hugh Dalton in November 1947, while cutting public expenditure elsewhere increased Dalton's quinquennial grant by more than 20 per cent to allow for inflation and other new demands, an action he later justified saying that 'it is on the advances that we make in scientific knowledge and on the energy, initiative, directive capacity and courage of these young graduates that the economic future of the country will largely depend'.[4]

Under R. A. Butler, Harold Macmillan and their successors at the Treasury the generosity to the universities continued. It was reinforced powerfully in 1963 by the report of the Robbins Committee on Higher Education, on which more below.

The magnitude of the increase in university funding is astonishing. In monetary terms the UGC recurrent grant was 50 times higher in 1972 than in 1946. Deflated by a combination of wages and prices, it had been increased 13 times.[5] As a percentage of GDP it had increased more than seven times. Since the GDP at constant prices had doubled, we arrive by this measure at a 15-fold increase.

But this was not all. Non-recurrent grants for capital expenditure, which were small before the war, were increased greatly as new universities were built

Table 7.1. UGC recurrent grant, deflated and as a % of GDP, 1946 to 1972

	Grant		Universities' cost index	Grant deflated index	Grant as % of GDP
	£ millions	index	index	index	GDP
1946	5.1	100	100	100	0.06
1951	15.2	298	125	230	0.12
1963	58.6	1,149	219	522	0.22
1972	254.4	4,988	378	1,319	0.45

3 Berdahl, *British Universities*, 74.
4 'News Report', *Universities Quarterly* 2 (1948): 215, cited in Berdahl, *British Universities*, 75 fn.
5 For 1963 to 1972 I have used the UPPI index, precursor of the HEPPI index; for the earlier periods I have combined a wage and price index.

and old ones were expanded and modernised. In the post-Robbins years 1964 to 1969 the recurrent grant averaged £126 million a year, the non-recurrent grant £60 million.[6]

The golden age was not unique to Britain. In other Western European countries the universities, as judged by the number of enrolments, were expanded as fast. According to Walter Ruegg, a leading historian of European universities, the common purpose was 'to increase competitiveness vis-à-vis the United States and the Soviet Union.'[7]

Of course causation was more complex than that and varied from country to country. In Britain three arguments were commonly made for spending more on universities: the life-enriching qualities of education and scholarship; the desire to increase social justice by widening access to university education; and the need to expand the physical sciences for the sake of the nation's military and industrial strength. One cannot know their relative importance. All one can say is that the rival political parties espoused higher education for reasons of this kind and backed it competitively: they engaged in what one might call consensual competition, arguing more about modalities than ends.

The favourable political tide would probably not have been translated so generously into money in the post-war years had it not been for the extraordinary way in which spending on the universities was administered by the UGC and the Treasury. Later, the rhetoric of the Robbins Report was so forceful that whatever the method of administration its recommendations would probably have been adopted.

The Role of the UGC

It will be remembered that under H. A. L. Fisher responsibility for government grants to the universities was placed in the hands of the UGC, a committee directly under the Treasury.[8] The committee's terms of reference were, 'To enquire into the financial needs of University education in the United Kingdom and to advise the Government as to the application of any grants that may be made by Parliament to meet them', meaning that (a) it should advise the Treasury how much was needed by the universities and (b) it should divide the money between the universities without interfering in how they spent it.

---

6 Kenneth S. Davies, Paul Walker, David Tupman, 'Universities, Numbers, Money, Policies, 1945–85', in W. A. C. Stewart, *Higher Education in Postwar Britain* (1989), 287.

7 Walter Ruegg (ed.), *A History of the University in Europe* (2011), IV: 14 and 43.

8 See Chapter 3.

This arrangement had the consequence, possibly unintended, that spending on the universities was not subjected to the scrutiny applied to other types of public expenditure. Under the normal procedure, the Board of Education would have submitted estimates of future expenditure on universities to the Treasury, and the Treasury would have scrutinised the figures and set about trying to cut them. Instead, the Treasury, since it helped to formulate the UGC's case, was in the position of sponsor as well as purse holder, of supplicant as well as benefactor: the usual adversarial negotiation was absent. Moreover, the senior Treasury officials who guided the decisions were generally high-flyers from Oxford and Cambridge who maintained connections with their college. A rather intimate elite ran the system, and did so efficiently as regards cost and time spent in bureaucratic formalities.

A conspicuous example is Sir Edward ('Eddie') Playfair (1909–1999), a Treasury knight who had been a scholar and was made an honorary fellow of King's, to which college he was devoted. His friend Noel Annan, provost of King's from 1956 to 1966, wrote in an obituary that at the Treasury Playfair, a man who liked dons, books and clever people like himself, had been responsible for the financing of the universities at the end of the 1939–45 war, and went on:

> Playfair realised that, as after the First World War, the universities would be flooded with returning warriors and in any case needed to expand. Although the Treasury is traditionally concerned with reining in public expenditure, Playfair relished being able to increase the subvention to learning.[9]

Annan was a person given to histrionic hyperbole, but he surely did not invent Playfair's views.[10] Hugh Dalton, the chancellor of the exchequer at the time, was also a Kingsman.

In the 1950s and 1960s the growth of the universities was strongly driven forward in different ways by two men of power from the academic world, Lord Murray and Lord Robbins. The first operated quietly within the machine, the second bombarded the body politic with one of the great state papers of the century.

Lord Murray (then Sir Keith Murray) was chairman of the UGC from 1953 to 1963. In his brilliant insider's account of the committee in this period,

---

9 Noel Annan, 'Obituary: Sir Edward Playfair', *Independent*, 25 March 1999.
10 Playfair gave a fascinating, considered account of the workings of the UGC and its relationship to the Treasury in evidence to the Select Committee on Estimates on 5 February 1952. See *Parliamentary Papers, 1951–52*, vol. 5.

John Carswell, a civil servant who over a long period served and observed the UGC from close to, said of Murray:

The effects of his period in office, though little noticed outside the university world, can hardly be exaggerated. In manner large, benevolent, persuasive, in action almost inexhaustible, he was a convinced and consistent expansionist. He was no delegator. Provided he had the facts and figures he could draft a blue-book of 200 pages singlehanded in a matter of weeks. He was a man for the times.[11]

In Murray's period in office the number of university students more than doubled and seven new universities were born.

Lord Robbins, a forceful and public person, was appointed by the government in February 1961 to preside over a review of the whole field of higher education. John Carswell described him thus:

When I first met him he impressed me as a bland silver lion, all mass and whiteness. His huge frame was surmounted by an enormous face and a mass of silvery hair. Along with his gentle manner one sensed a giant paw from which a claw or two would sometimes make a carefully modulated appearance. I have never met anyone except Otto who was more confident that he was right.[12] It was a friendly, comforting confidence, and disagreement was tolerated: but made no impression.

There was a certain simplicity of mind about Robbins, which dogged his great abilities and magnificent personality. He loved government, and thought he understood its ways, so he was easily captivated by forms and structures. He saw before him noble high principles and noble goals, and was liable to wave aside brutal or inconvenient realities. He saw, correctly, that a moment had come in the history of higher education at which mere endorsement of official advice would fall short of the occasion. He intended from the first that his report should mark a great advance.[13]

With his civil servant's knowledge, Carswell tells us the Robbins Committee was created mainly because the universities had grown so much in cost,

---

11 John Carswell, *Government and the Universities in Britain: Programme and Performance 1960–1980* (1985), 14.
12 The reference is to Sir Richard ('Otto') Clarke (1910–1975), a Treasury knight of extraordinary speed of mind and impulsive certainty of opinion, described by Carswell earlier in his book; father of Charles Clarke, the Labour politician of today.
13 Carswell, *Government and the Universities*, 27–8.

number and complexity, and consequently had aroused so much interest in Parliament and the media, that their governance could no longer be handled comfortably by the informal UGC–Treasury system. Hence the committee's terms of reference invited it to focus particularly on improved forms of organisation:

> ...to review the pattern of full-time higher education in Great Britain and in the light of national needs and resources to advise Her Majesty's Government on what principles its long term development should be based. In particular, to advise, in the light of these principles, whether there should be any change in that pattern, whether any new types of institution are desirable and whether any modifications should be made in the present arrangements for planning and co-ordinating the development of the various types of institution.[14]

The Robbins Report

Regardless of this guidance Robbins, ex cathedra, made his mark by asserting '...as an axiom that courses of higher education should be available for all those who are qualified by ability and attainment to pursue them and wish to do so', and by laying out a numerical programme for the rapid pursuit of that grand objective. The programme was embedded in a most impressive, fluent display of reasoning and opinions about the benefits and problems of higher education, accompanied by excellent statistical analysis of the existing system.

The figures for the number of places that would be required to satisfy the Robbins axiom were arrived at by estimating how many 18-year-olds would seek places in the years ahead. This was done by:

1. estimating the number of 18-year-olds coming forward each year, which could be done with confidence up to 1980 since they were already born;
2. assuming that the proportion of each year's cohort that became eligible to apply for higher education by gaining two or more to passes at A levels would continue to rise as it had done since 1954, which meant it would go from 7 per cent in 1961 to 12.9 per cent in 1980;
3. assuming by reference to experience abroad that, of those who thus became eligible, the proportion that would apply for a place in higher education would increase from 60 to 66 per cent by 1980.

---

14 *Higher Education: Report of the Committee appointed by the Prime Minister under the Chairmanship of Lord Robbins, 1961–63* (Cmnd. 2154; October 1963), 4. Henceforth, *Robbins Report.*

The results, after estimates of overseas students and postgraduates had been added, were these (Table 7.2):

Table 7.2. Robbins Committee estimates of the required number of student places[15]

	1962–3 actual	1980–81 estimated	Increase
All higher education			
Home students only	195,000	507,000	× 2.6
Home and overseas students	216,000	558,000	× 2.6
Of which, universities	130,000	346,000	× 2.7

As regards the cost, it was estimated that expenditure on higher education would have to be increased from 0.8 per cent of GDP to 1.6 or 1.9 per cent (depending on the rate of growth of GDP). It was taken for granted that this would all be paid for by the government and local authorities. Two alternative means of financing were addressed, but no reliance was placed upon them.

Of fund-raising, the report said: 'We should like to state emphatically that the assumption of extended responsibility by the state has not made benefactions any less desirable or deprived them of their *raison d'être*', and went on with a short orotund discussion of their merits.[16]

Student loans were considered at rather greater length, but were rejected on the grounds that at a time when many parents were just beginning to contemplate higher education for their children, especially girls, loans might deter them. But loans were not quite ruled out for ever: 'if, as times goes on, the habit [of sending children to university] is more firmly established, the arguments of justice in distribution and of the advantage of increasing individual responsibility may come to weigh more heavily and lead to some experiment in this direction.'[17]

The possibility that the committee's estimates of the required number of places, if adopted, might produce more trained and educated persons than were needed, was answered by citing advice the committee had received when visiting the Soviet Union: in the Soviet Union, there would always be use for people who had been trained to the limit of their ability. Remarkably, the report goes on: 'We do not believe the Soviet Union is the only country that can make full use of the brains of its people. This country above all must do so: if regard is paid to Great Britain's relative lack of natural resources it

---

15 *Robbins Report*, tables 28, 30 and 44.
16 *Robbins Report*, para. 658.
17 *Robbins Report*, para. 647.

would be a grave risk to aim any lower than we recommend.'[18] At another point they say that their estimates for 1980–81 'will mark the dawn of a new era in British higher education'.[19]

These passages are a reminder of the political values of the early 1960s. They are imbued by belief in the duty and power of the state to improve society; and they take for granted that the nation will willingly countenance a doubling or more of public expenditure on higher education. (The share of GDP then taken in taxation was not far different from what it is now, but the top rate of income tax was 88.75 per cent.[20]) They are not the sentiments of a socialist: Lord Robbins, after a brief fit of socialism in his youth, was a liberal conservative, appointed by a Conservative government, and the members of his commission were representative of the great and the good of the period.

John Carswell tells us that the report

> ...was produced under increasing pressure that it should be ready in time for the coming general election. There was nothing wrong with this at all. Higher education was a burning issue. No doubt an advantage was hoped for by the Conservatives then in power, with their slogan 'Modernisation of Britain', but their opponents were no less committed and the general interest made it absolutely right that the Report should be before the country when it came to vote.

The Cost

The cost to the government of higher education before and after the Robbins Report had two components: the subsidy to the universities and other institutions of higher education to sustain them as providers of teaching and research; and the subsidy to students to support their living costs. In 1960 a committee under Sir Colin Anderson recommended that a tangle of post-war grants for living costs, of which 90 per cent of students were beneficiaries, should by replaced by a single comprehensive system of grants administered by local authorities, funded by a combination of local rates and the central government. The scheme, which was predicated on a much smaller population of students than Robbins was to advocate, was carried into law (with the grants subject to means testing) while the Robbins Committee was at work.

---

18 *Robbins Report*, para. 194.
19 *Robbins Report*, para. 181.
20 The standard rate in 1962–63 was 7s 9p, the top surtax rate 10s in the pound. Earned income relief exempted a limited amount of earned income from tax but did not reduce the top rate. *Report of the Commissioners of Inland Revenue for the year ended 31 March 1963* (1964).

In short, the Anderson Committee said that everyone who could get into full-time education should have a grant for living costs, while the Robbins Report said that everyone who wanted higher education and achieved two A levels should be provided with it free. The consequence was a large bill.[21]

For the years immediately ahead, the size of the bill was much amplified by a bulge in the number of boys and girls reaching 18 years of age, consequent on the baby boom after the war. Under the heading 'The short-term emergency' it was estimated that over the five years from 1963 to 1968 the number places in universities would need to be increased 48 per cent, and the number in other higher education by 52 per cent.[22] Under the heading 'The crisis immediately ahead', the closing words the summary of the Robbins Report, were:

> In our judgement, this is an emergency of the same importance as the emergency produced by demobilisation after the last war and demanding the same type of extraordinary measures to meet it. If the needs of this situation are not adequately met by immediate government action, many of our plans for long term expansion will be seriously endangered.

The Robbins recommendations for expansion were accepted and very largely executed in the 1960s and 1970s. But at the end of the 1970s the golden age came to an end. The post-war consensus on the role of the state on which the report was founded broke down under the impact of inflation, economic crises and Mrs Thatcher.

The End of the Golden Age

In the new era, Conservative and Labour governments, and now the coalition government, have:

1. cut expenditure on universities in fits and starts;
2. sought to make universities behave as enterprises that produce education and research to meet the needs of business;
3. urged universities to seek private money by fund-raising, seeking private research contracts, obtaining royalties from patented innovations, fostering spin-off enterprises or by any other means; and
4. re-introduced tuition fees, first for foreign students and now, accompanied by loans, for home students.

---

21 Carswell, *Government and the Universities*, 25.
22 *Robbins Report*, Table 61, 260.

The abandonment of the Robbins axiom that higher education should be provided free has been widely unpopular since it means that the children of all classes, including the influential middle class, will have to pay fees to a greater or lesser degree. That reliance should again be placed on fees was recommended strongly in two reports – the Dearing Report and the Browne Report – the first commissioned by the Conservatives, the second by New Labour.[23]

There has been remarkably little public protest by academics against the growing infringement of the principle that the universities should be independent of government intervention, though Oxford seems to have been more vocal about it than Cambridge.

The Growth of State Interference

It was probably inevitable that since governments had come to provide so much money to the universities they would want to have a greater say than before on how it was spent. That has happened step by step.

In the 1980s, by which time the UGC was allocating a huge but tightened budget amongst a mixed bag of old universities, new universities and colleges of advanced technology (CATs), it had to be more selective than before; and it needed to be able openly to justify its actions to governments and parliaments that were more critical than before of public spending. A criterion was needed for allocating money that would command respect. The one chosen by the UGC was research performance. The choice was advantageous to Cambridge, a great centre of research, but it resulted in periodic government inspections of university research in order to assess how large a grant should be awarded to each department. These inspections have become a major intrusion into the independence of Cambridge and other universities; they have long been criticised for rewarding quantity not quality, since they rely heavily on counting the number of works published; and for imposing implicit priorities as between subjects and between research and teaching.

The main steps by which government intervention has been introduced have been these:

1. 1964: Before Labour came to power, the UGC was transferred from the Treasury to the Department of Education and Science, then under Quintin Hogg (later Lord Hailsham); a main component of H. A. L. Fisher's bulwark against state intervention in the universities was thus removed. (Despite criticism, his successor, Anthony Crosland, who favoured

---

23 *Report of the National Committee of Inquiry into Higher Education* (1997); and *Securing a sustainable future for higher education: an independent review of higher education funding and student finance* (2010).

comprehensive schools, adopted the dual system whereby polytechnics and other vocational colleges were to be developed and financed via the local authorities (with central government support), while the universities were to continue under the UGC–Treasury regime.)

2. 1974: The quinquennial grant for the universities was abolished in favour of an annual grant.

3. 1988: The UGC was abolished and replaced by the University Funding Council (UFC), on which only 7 out of 15 members were academics, the rest mostly businessmen. The local authorities' power over the polytechnics and other vocational colleges was severely reduced, and a Polytechnic and Colleges Funding Council (PCFC) was created though which the polytechnics and other vocational colleges were now to be funded.[24]

4. 1992: The UFC and part of the PCFC were merged and the allocation of grants for all higher education was handed to a single body, the Higher Education Funding Council for England (HEFCE), and to parallel bodies for Wales, Scotland and Northern Ireland: a fully centralised system of funding and control was thus established.[25] The rump of the PCFC was re-christened the Further Education Funding Council (FEFC). The polytechnics and local authority colleges were re-christened universities: the number of the 'university' students in the UK was apparently doubled at a stroke (Chart 7.1).

John Major, the prime minister at the time, implies in his autobiography that this reclassification of polytechnics and local authority colleges as 'universities' was introduced on his initiative for the sake of technical education. (What the effect has been on technical training I have not explored.) His words were these:

> For forty years we had failed to give technical education the attention it needed, and I wanted to put this right – to bring academic and vocational training closer, without fusing them or diluting academic quality.[26]

The 1992 Act was an important step in state interference for two related reasons:

1. It contains no reference to the independence of the universities, a principle so long proclaimed by governments and defended by the old universities. The omission may be read as a manifestation of the general political trend

---

24 Education Reform Act 1988.
25 Further and Higher Education Act 1992.
26 John Major, *The Autobiography* (1999), 396.

towards managerial intervention from the centre, and also as a consequence of the amalgamation of the polytechnics with the universities: it could not be said that the independence appropriate to great seats of learning was appropriate to institutions that provide vocational training to meet the needs of the surrounding economy. The latter should be told what to provide, though it seems questionable whether that guidance should be provided by the central government rather than by local government.

2. The dictates of equality of treatment for all the 'universities', as now defined, has inevitably meant that Cambridge and other 'old' universities have been subjected to regulation appropriate to institutions whose main task is vocational training.

Chart 7.1. Government grants and number of students at UK 'universities', 1921–2009

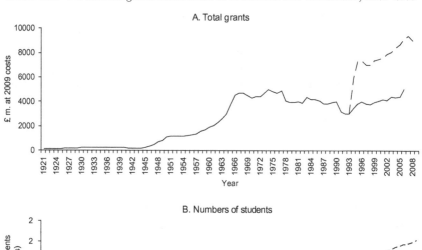

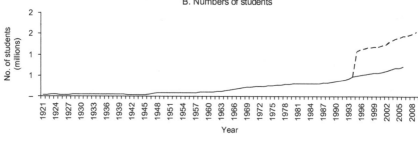

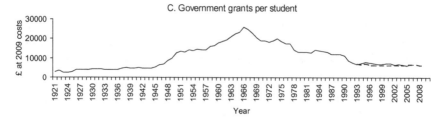

The annual reports of HEFCE, which make no mention of the independence of the universities, have come to consist of statements in management-speak of 'Our Mission' and 'Our Strategic Aims', expressed in the manner of business objectives dictated and enforced from the centre. They devote much space to describing numerous Key Performance Targets (KPTs) and their assessment of the progress they have made towards achieving them in all the numerous institutions of higher education for which they are responsible, all described in a self-congratulatory style, redolent with such phrases as 'delivering our core functions' and 'the improving trend of stakeholder satisfaction'.[27]

Periodic inspections of the quality of teaching were introduced by HEFCE in obedience to the 1992 Act, for which purpose it created a private agency, the Quality Assurance Agency (QAA), partly paid for by the universities. The Research Assessment Exercise became inflated with instructions and formulae as HEFCE applied it to the many and varied institutions under its command. For example, paragraph 156 of the guidance booklet for the 2008 RAE said:

> RA5a will have a length limit. We will decide this limit in the context of the criteria statements drawn up by panels. We do not expect it to be less than the combined limit for RA5 and RA6 in the 2001 RAE (that is, four A4 sides for submissions of up to six FTE staff, eight A4 sides for submissions of between six and 20 FTE staff, and one additional A4 side for each additional set of 20 FTEs up to a maximum of 14 sides). We will publish the limit alongside the panel's final published criteria statements.

In 2006 the RAE was replaced by a new system called the Research Excellence Framework (REF) intended to lighten the burden on academics. In the words of a HEFCE press release put out at the end of 2006:

> For subjects in science, engineering, technology and medicine (SET) the quality indicator will be a bibliometric statistic relating to research publications or citations. For other subjects, the quality indicator will continue to involve a lighter touch expert review of research outputs, with a substantial reduction in the administrative burden.[28]

Then in the last days of the Labour government the task of the REF was changed 'so as to reward the quality of researchers' contribution to public

27 See, for example, Higher Education Funding Council for England, *Annual report and accounts 2009–10*, www.hefce.ac.uk.
28 HEFCE press release of 6 December 2006.

policy-making and to public engagement', as well as research excellence.[29] To achieve that end HEFCE announced in October 2009 that research excellence would now be assessed by three criteria: 'Outputs', 'Impact' and 'Environment'.[30] The definitions of these words given by HEFCE are so woolly that is it difficult to see how they can be applied.

At first sight it is surprising that governments have intervened in our universities more as they have given them less. One might expect intervention to be greater when giving, and hence dependence is greater, and vice versa. But what we are observing is a manifestation of a national political phenomenon, namely the extraordinary increase in regulation that has been introduced in recent decades by governments of all parties while they claim to be reducing government and liberating enterprise and choice.[31] Another possible explanation may be relevant: when a giver is generous, the recipients may be little inclined to question the fairness of his (or her) gifts; but when money is tight, the giver will have to be selective and the recipients may be more likely to question the fairness of his gifts and how he decides upon them: he may be driven to make and announce rules.

In her memoirs published in 1993, Mrs Thatcher recounts that in her last days as prime minister she came to feel that intervention in the old universities had gone too far, and that she was planning to liberate them:

> I had to concede that these critics [those genuinely concerned about the future autonomy of and academic integrity of universities] had a stronger case than I would have liked. It made me concerned that many distinguished academics thought that Thatcherism meant a philistine subordination of scholarship to the immediate requirements of vocational training. That was certainly no part of my kind of Thatcherism. That was why before I left office Brian Griffiths, with my encouragement, had started working on a scheme to give the leading universities much more independence.[32]

---

29 Letter of 21 January 2009, headed 'Higher Education Funding 2009–10', from the Right Hon. John Denham to Tim Mellville-Ross, chairman of HEFCE, www.hefce.ac.uk.

30 'The Research Excellence Framework: A brief guide to the proposals', October 2009, www.hefce.ac.uk.

31 For an excellent description of the development of intervention in the universities in Mrs Thatcher's time see: Simon Jenkins, *Accountable to None: the Tory Nationalization of Britain* (1995), chap. 7.

32 Margaret Thatcher, *The Downing Street Years* (1993), 599. Brian Griffiths, now Lord Griffiths of Fforestfach and a banker, was her policy adviser. Simon Jenkins, *Accountable to None*, 142, suggests that the draconic treatment of the universities in the early 1980s by Mrs Thatcher and Nigel Lawson, her chancellor of the exchequer, was an expression of

One wonders what she has thought of the rampant growth of interference in the universities brought about by her successors of all parties.

Fees Revived

In the golden age tuition was provided free to undergraduates (not postgraduates) regardless of the income of their parents and their nationality, and it was paid for by the government through the current grant. Consequently, tuition fees, having provided about 40 per cent of the university's income before the war, provided only 7 per cent in 1966 (Table 7.4).

Since then fee income, deflated by costs, has increased fourfold, a substantial increase but less than that in other types of income, notably research grants and commercial income. The restoration of fees has come in two main phases. In the first, tuition fees were imposed on foreign students, in the second on home students.

When the Conservatives, led by Mrs Thatcher, came to power in 1979 committed to a policy of fiscal retrenchment, they cut the grant to the universities, applied restrictive quotas on the number of home students, and in 1980 announced that overseas students, who like home students had received free tuition, should henceforth be charged fees that at least covered costs.[33] The effect of the high fees on overseas students who were poor was mitigated by some government money and, at Cambridge, by the remarkable fund-raising efforts of Dr Seal on behalf of Commonwealth students and others. Students from EU countries have necessarily been treated like UK students.

These measures gave British universities a strong financial incentive to admit more overseas students, and permitted them to do so without limit at a time when they were in search of new sources of money and when, moreover, there was a rapid growth in overseas demand for places at UK universities, generated by rising incomes abroad and the opening up of cheap international

Table 7.3. Fees as a percentage of the university's income, 1913 to 2009

1913	1920	1939	1946	1966	1986	2009
54	45	38	11	7	14	12

anger with the universities provoked, *inter alia*, by a letter from 364 academic economists criticising her economic policy (of which my colleague, Frank Hahn, and I, were the authors).

33 *House of Commons Debates*, 6 May 1980, vol. 984, col. 3–4.

communication and travel. The result, probably unintended, was an influx of foreign students accompanied by a boost to income from fees, the magnitude of which has varied from one university to another.

On average about 20 per cent of students at UK universities now come from outside the UK; of these about one third come from the EU, two thirds from 'overseas', with the figure much higher for postgraduates than for undergraduates. The percentages are lower at the former polytechnics than at the 'old universities', which generally enjoy greater international prestige and have greater strength in research. An exceptionally high proportion of overseas students – 48 per cent and 58 per cent – is to be found at the London School of Economics and the London Business School.[34] Both probably attract many good overseas applicants, and both may have been influenced in two ways by being schools that specialise in economics: their response to financial incentives may be sharper than that of the average multi-discipline university; and, unlike those at multi-disciplinary universities, they do not have to worry about upsetting the balance amongst subjects and so losing universality if they admit too many students of economics and related subjects. Moreover, the London Business School takes only postgraduates.

Cambridge responded without inhibition to the incentive to take more overseas students. A report on how it planned to respond to the government cuts stated that: 'On the side of increases in income, one of the main objectives is to increase the number of overseas students admitted to the University'.[35] But the Cambridge procedures for admitting students may have blunted the incentive to take overseas students. Decisions to admit undergraduates are made by the colleges, which benefit little from the high university fees for overseas

Table 7.4. Foreign students as percentage of students admitted to Cambridge

	1980–81	2008–09
UK	89	62
EU	3	13
Overseas	8	24

Source: Student numbers 2008–09, *Cambridge University Reporter*, Special no. 4, 8 October 2009, Table 6; and estimates of the breakdown for 1980–81 supplied by the Cambridge University Student Statistics Office.

---

34 HEFCE statistics of overseas student numbers, available from www.hefce.ac.uk.
35 'Report of the Council of the Senate on the financial position of the Chest for the years 1980–81 to 1982–83', *Cambridge University Reporter*, 16 June 1982, 673.

students: they go principally to the university. In the case of postgraduates, who are admitted by colleges in consultation with the departments and faculties, the procedure for allocating extra fee income amongst the departments and faculties, which is complex, must also have diminished the incentive. Nevertheless, the proportion of overseas students has trebled and the proportion of EU students has more than quadrupled since 1981. Non-UK students (those in the EU and overseas categories) now make up nearly 40 per cent of undergraduates and postgraduates admitted to Cambridge.

The second phase of retrenchment – the raising of fees for home students – has been in play for some years, but only with the coming to power of the Conservative–Liberal coalition in 2010, again an incoming government committed to fiscal retrenchment, has a step been taken that will substantially increase fee income. While the government subsidy has been cut, the universities have now been permitted to raise undergraduate fees to a maximum of £9,000 a year accompanied by student loans, on the condition that they provide some bursaries for those in need. Cambridge has decided to charge the full £9,000, as have other universities that are confident that they will not lack applicants at that price. It is forecast that between 2008–09 and 2011–12 the proportion of the university's income that comes from fees will rise from 12 to 15 per cent (Table 8.2).

The contrast with conditions before the 1939–45 war is remarkable. The demand for places was then so weak that, despite the minimal qualifications required for admission, almost anyone whose family could afford the fees could get into a Cambridge college as an undergraduate. Now demand, which comes from all parts of a much richer world, vastly exceeds supply.

Chapter 8

INCOME AND EXPENDITURE SINCE 1945

Since 1945 the university's income has gone through three phases: rapid growth fed by government money; slow growth as the flow of government money was cut; and a recovery in growth as more money was obtained from sources other than the British government. Now a new phase of government cuts has been entered, as a result of which the total income of the university, deflated by costs, ceased growing in 2010 and is forecast to decline.

Summary estimates of income for the beginning and end of the three periods, deflated by costs, are given in Table 8.1. Because of difficulties in consolidating the earlier accounts, comparability between the years may not have been perfectly achieved, and the years selected may not mark precisely the turning points between the periods.[1] But the possible errors are small relative to the changes observed.

The changing importance of the different sources of the university's income is shown in Table 8.2.

The main points to note are:

1. The increase in the university's total income, adjusted for inflation, has been far greater than the increase in student numbers, principally because the expanding physical sciences have required and obtained increasingly expensive facilities.
2. The general government grant, having provided 71 per cent of the university's income in 1966, provided only 28 per cent in 2009, a slightly smaller proportion than in 1946, and it is still falling (Table 8.2).
3. The largest recent gain in Cambridge's income has been in research grants and research contracts obtained from institutions other than the

---

1 Many streams of income, for example income from trusts and grants to departments, that had come into existence by 1946 were not consolidated with the accounts of the University Chest till 1962; and since then the basis of consolidation has been changed.

Table 8.1. The university's income, deflated by costs, and student numbers, 1946 to 2009

Indices	1946	1966	1986	2009
University's non-governmental income	100	177	337	1724
Government grants etc.	100	662	752	1483
Total	100	434	531	1622
Student numbers	*100*	*149*	*188*	*261*

Table 8.2. The changing pattern of the university's income, 1946 to 2012

	Percentages of total income				
	1946	1966	1986	2009	Forecast 2012
Government general grants	30	71	52	28	24
Government research grants/contracts	18	6	15	15	16
Other research grants etc.	Neg.	4	8	20	23
Endowment income, including trusts	32	9	6	6	6
Fees	11	7	14	12	15
Contribution from colleges	7	2	0	0	0
Other	2	1	6	18	16
Total	100	100	100	100	100
All research grants/contracts	16	10	23	35	39
College endowment income as % of					
a. university's endowment income	194	207	408	151	n.a.
b. university total income	62	19	23	10	n.a.

Source: Appendix 8A.

UK government. In 2009 20 per cent of income came from this new source of income.

4. There was also a big increase in income from various commercial activities (included under 'Other' in Table 8.2).

5. Student fees, having declined in importance in the golden age, have been partially revived and are now being increased.

6. Since 1986 endowment income, having been left behind in the golden age, has just kept up with the growth of other kinds of income.

7. The colleges no longer contribute directly to the university. The university contribution scheme introduced in the 1880s now serves only to transfer money from rich to poor colleges.

The following paragraphs look more closely at the growth of research grants, at the investment of the university's endowment fund, and at fund-raising, in all of which cases performance has depended primarily on actions by the university, not the government.

The Transformation of Research Grants

The pattern of research grants today is extremely different from what it was in the inter-war years. Then nearly all grants received by Cambridge came from the government, and 70 per cent or more were for agricultural research (Chapter 3). Now the Agricultural Research Council no longer exists, and agriculture research receives little money.

In seeking to make universities concentrate more on commercially oriented research, governments have made successive changes to the organisation and naming of the research councils. For example, the Science Research Council has become the Engineering and Science Research Council (ESRC), and the Agricultural Research Council became the Agricultural and Food Research Council before it was wound down and subsumed into other bodies. This turbulence impedes the tracing from past to present of the flow of research council money to particular subjects. But the main development since 1946 is clear: a huge increase in the flow of research money into biology and medicine. This has been, for Cambridge at least, the great growth area of research.

In 2009, nearly £140 million, which is just over half the money the university received by way of research grants and contracts, went to biology and medicine (Table 8.3). Nearly half of this came from UK charities.

Table 8.3. The importance of biology and medicine in the university's research grants and contracts, 2009

Source	Biology and medicine	Total	Biology and medicine as % of total
	£ million		
UK research councils	40.3	112.5	36
UK charitable bodies	64.5	72.1	89
UK govt. bodies, incl. health	12.1	18.1	67
UK industry and commerce	3.7	17.9	21
EU govt. bodies	8.6	18.4	47
Non-UK charities	5.2	6.5	80
Non-UK industry	1.0	6.4	16
Other	3.5	8.2	43
Total	138.9	260.1	53

Source: Higher Education Statistics Agency.

The Wellcome Trust alone provided £36 million, a sum almost as great as that provided to biology and medicine by government research councils; Cancer Research UK provided £14 million; the big drug companies provided lesser sums.

Not included in these figures is the huge amount of money that is put into biological and medical research by the many research institutions, public and private, that cluster around the university. The Medical Research Council, which financed the work of Kendrew, Perutz, Crick and Watson, and other fathers of molecular biology, now puts £30 million a year into its Laboratory of Molecular Biology – and puts money into other units in Cambridge. The Sanger Institute, created by the Wellcome Trust in 1993 to play a leading part in the Human Genome Project, has an income of about £80 million a year, and the Babraham Institute for life sciences research, created in 1948, has an income of about £20 million, most of it from the Biotechnology and Biological Sciences Research Council.

Of the many laboratories where biological and medical research is pursued, some are charitable institutions, many are commercial enterprises housed on the numerous science and business parks around Cambridge. Their connections with the university are various. For example, a scientist from the Laboratory of Molecular Biology may hold a college fellowship. Scientists from the research institutions, the university and the colleges, nowadays engage, with the encouragement of their employers, in the commercial development of their ideas through the licensing of inventions and the formation of high-tech companies.

Two reasons why charitable money has been so strongly concentrated on biological and medical research suggest themselves. Firstly, the discovery of the genetic code opened up huge opportunities for research that is intellectually exciting and rewarding in the field of molecular biology. Secondly, those who create charities and those who give to them have been attracted by the prospect that biological and medical research will alleviate human suffering and may cure diseases that they themselves fear.

The government research council from which most money came to Cambridge in 2009 (£41 million) was that for the engineering and physical sciences.[2] These subjects received a considerable amount from industry, British and foreign, usually in sums of moderate size; a substantial proportion came from the petroleum industry and from the military and aerospace industry. Charitable bodies provided little, presumably because engineering and the physical sciences do not arouse feelings of charity. But commercial ventures

---

2 Financial Management Information for the year ended 31 July 2009, *Cambridge University Reporter*, 21 January 2010, 73.

that exploit the physical sciences, notably electronics, have proliferated, like those in the biomedical sciences, on the science and business parks around Cambridge.

Endowment Income

The evolution of endowment income can be attributed to two causes: how successfully the university has invested its capital, and how much it has increased its capital by obtaining gifts, spontaneous and solicited. In other words, it can be attributed to investment performance and fund-raising performance. In both domains the university has in recent years adopted American practices. The result so far has not been a rich harvest: endowment income is still a rather small fraction of total income. The following paragraphs look at the evolution of investment policy and fund-raising.

Investment Policy

In 1958 the university pooled the long-term capital of its many endowments, including trusts, in a single fund so as to simplify management and accounting. Since that date it has been possible to judge the university's investment performance by comparing the change in the value of a unit in that fund (the CUEF – Cambridge University Endowment Fund) with the change in various financial yardsticks. In Charts 8.1 and 8.2 I have compared the value of a unit in the CUEF with a UK share price index and with the performance of Trinity College's Amalgamated Trusts Fund, which is comparable to the CUEF, as well as with the retail price index.[3] From the first chart, which is on a log scale, it can be seen that:

a. Since 1958 the CUEF has kept pace with the share price index; Trinity's fund has done exceptionally well and outpaced it.
b. Whereas the market trend was upwards till about 2000, it has been flat since then; but retail prices have moved upwards.

From the chart on a linear scale it can be seen that in the past decade the market has been volatile.

The university's performance looks respectable: to keep up in the long run with the share price index relevant to one's economic setting is a sound objective for any investor.

---

3 FT 30 index up to 1962, thereafter FT all-share index, taken from the *Barclays Equity Gilt Study 2011*, available via www.barcap.com/egs/.

Chart 8.1. Investment performance of the CUEF, 1958–2009

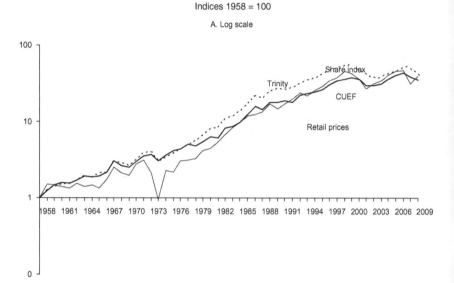

Chart 8.2. Investment performance of the CUEF, 1991–2010

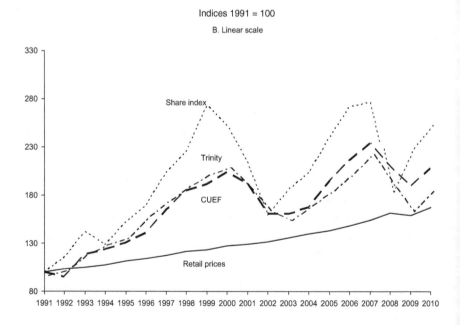

In 2005 the university, following the example of some American universities, adopted a more adventurous investment policy, which it describes thus:[4]

> The CUEF is managed on a total return basis, such that the amount distributed for budgetary expenditure is determined by a formula which has regard to the total return reasonably to be expected in the long run. The CUEF's portfolio is invested to maximise total investment return and a substantial proportion of the underlying investments yield little or no income in the form of dividends, interest and rents.

In plain words, this means that capital gains as well as income are to be pursued and spent. It is a policy that does not necessitate more risk-taking but opens the door to it: it is permissive in that it means that capital can be spent, and it is seductive in that it invites risk-taking in the pursuit of short-run capital gains. In the United States it brought rich rewards to some universities in recent decades when the stock market was doing well and, in one case at least, severe financial distress when the stock market collapsed.[5]

Table 8.4. The recent performance of the CUEF

Year to 31 July	Capital £000	Funds introduced £000	Number of units 000	Net income £000	Capital per unit £	Income per unit £	Distribution per unit £
2001	702,387	19,074	23,571	25,682	29.80	1.08	1.24
2002	590,478	3,786	23,701	25,921	24.91	1.09	1.27
2003	595,623	5,093	23,910	22,423	24.91	0.94	1.30
2004	643,865	21,948	24,754	21,845	26.01	0.88	1.04
2005	747,316	859	24,742	28,524	30.20	1.15	1.10
2006	870,810	40,805	25,914	26,035	33.60	1.00	1.14
2007	990,788	47,378	27,228	31,696	36.39	1.16	1.21
2008	906,513	21,189	27,810	31,293	32.60	1.12	1.30
2009	953,863	136,308	32,498	16,022	29.35	0.49	1.40
2010	1,142,613	93,500	35,389	7,458	32.29	0.21	1.41
2011	1,550,396	305,941	44,360	..	34.95	..	1.45

Source: *Cambridge University Reporter*, 18 January 2011, 82, and 21 December 2011, 53.

---

4 'Report of the Council on distributions from the Amalgamated Fund', *Cambridge University Reporter*, 15 December 2004; and Grace of 9 February 2005, approved 18 February 2005.

5 In Britain the abolition in 1997 of dividend tax credits for charities and pension funds increased the attractions of capital gains relative to dividends.

Until about 2008 there was little change in investment policy, but since then the pursuit of total returns has been achieved by a major increase in reliance on capital gains. Table 8.4 shows that by 2010 the net income per unit of the fund had been reduced to less than one-fifth of its former value. Since more than 60 per cent of the fund was still allocated to equities, the large fall in income must have been caused by a major shift from equities that pay dividends into equities that retain their profits and plough them back in the pursuit of further growth and capital gains (Table 8.5). Ten per cent or so had been put into hedge funds.

So far the new policy has done well. From 2008 to 2011, the total return of the CUEF outpaced the total return on UK shares by an average of rather more than 1 per cent a year. This may be partly because CUEF is partly invested abroad.

Table 8.5. The asset allocation of the CUEF at 31 July 2010 and 2011, percentages

Type of asset	Percentages	
	2010	2011
Global equities	63	65
Private investment	2	3
Hedge funds etc. ('absolute return')	11	12
Credit	6	3
Property etc.	13	13
Fixed interest and cash	6	4
Total	100	100

Source: *Cambridge University Reporter*, 18 January 2011, 92, and 21 December 2011, 53.

Table 8.6. Comparison of the CUEF with the FT All-share Index

	Per cent change in total return, years ending 31 July				
	2008	2009	2010	2011	4 years to 2011
CUEF	− 6.8	− 5.7	+ 14.8	+ 12.7	+ 11.3
FT ASI	− 13.3	− 10.5	+ 19.3	+ 15.0	+ 6.4

Fund-Raising

As we saw in Chapter 4, active fund-raising by the university was given up at the approach of the 1939–45 war. The Cambridge University Association (CUA), founded in 1899, was allowed to die. With government money abundant, and charitable giving in the shadows as the state provided comprehensive welfare services, the flow of gifts fell away in the 1960s.

Following the turn of the political tide under Mrs Thatcher, fund-raising was revived. The government encouraged the universities to seek charitable money as an alternative to government money as the political ethos became more favourable to charitable giving, and in 1990 the government introduced Gift Aid, a general system of tax relief for charitable gifts. A further incentive was recently introduced when the Labour government announced that it would put £200 million over the years 2008–2011 into a 'matching funds scheme' in order to encourage private fund-raising by universities. Those institutions of higher education that had so far done little fund-raising would receive £1 for every pound they raised; most would receive £1 for every £2 raised; and those most advanced in fund-raising, including Oxford and Cambridge, would receive £1 for every £3 raised.[6]

In this setting, one university after another has set about fund-raising. The method used has been very different from that adopted a century earlier by the Cambridge University Association which we described in Chapter 2. Then patrician grandees led the way at Cambridge, as they did at Oxford, with an appeal for endowments that had little success. Between the wars businessmen, particularly those from new science-based industries, became prominent, seeking and giving considerable sums to Cambridge for subjects in which they had an interest (Chapter 4). Throughout the life of the CUA its expenses did not exceed the cost of one secretary, plus postage, printing and the like. Most of the work was done voluntarily.

Now fund-raising for universities in Britain is a rapidly growing, well-paid business, engaged in by persons who earn their money by raising, and promising to raise, money. For that purpose they apply practices and language that were evolved at American universities: they cultivate 'alumni';[7] they describe themselves as 'development directors' (as if they were responsible for planning the policies of their university); and they have an association, the Ross Group of Development Directors, that was formed in 2003 out of a previous Development Directors' Forum. This group has links with the Council for Advancement and Support of Education (CASE), a Washington-based association of university fund-raisers formed in 1974 that now has branches in London, Singapore and Mexico City and declares

---

6 See 'Matched funding scheme for voluntary giving 2008–2011', HEFCE Circular Letter 11/2008, 12 May 2008.

7 A term long used in the United States to describe ex-pupils but, until American-style fund-raising came in, rarely used in Britain, where 'old boys' and 'old girls' were used.

itself to be 'one of the world's largest non-profit educational associations in terms of institutional membership'.[8] Together these two organisations have since 2006–7 commissioned an annual Ross–CASE Survey of Gifts and Costs of Voluntary Giving which 'evaluates the philanthropic health of universities in the UK'.[9] These surveys, in which 98 per cent of UK universities participated in 2009–10, are valuable for their comprehensive and well-presented statistics of money raised by different methods, the costs incurred and similar matters, but as a 'philanthropic health check' they are less satisfactory. That is not surprising. When institutions, whether industrial companies, banks, trades unions, professional associations, charities or anything else, report what they have achieved and what they have spent, they tend to accentuate the positive and minimise, if not eliminate, the negative.

Notable points from the 2009–10 survey are:

1. In 2009–10, UK universities with fund-raising programmes employed just over 1,500 staff (or full-time equivalents); in two years the number employed had increased from 1,200, i.e. by a quarter. They spent £100 million, of which £71 million went on fund-raising, £22 million on alumni relations and £8 million on alumni magazines. The figures exclude universities that had started fund-raising in the previous three years and so were deemed to be starting up.

2. The total secured by the universities in 'new philanthropic funds', including pledges to give in the future, was £600 million; excluding pledges, the total was £500 million.

3. The median 'fund-raising expenditure per pound secured in the last three years' had declined from 32p to 23p since 2007–08 as new fund-raising programmes had begun to bring in money.

4. Oxford and Cambridge accounted for 50 per cent of the new funds secured by UK universities in the year.

These figures require qualification:

1. As the report concedes, the figures are not a measure of what has been brought in by fund-raisers, since it cannot be said how much would have

---

8 www.case.org/about-case.html.

9 www.natcen.ac.uk/media/674968/2009-10-report.pdf. In the UK there is also an Institute of Fundraising that reports trends and offers advice about fund-raising for charities in all fields (www.institute-of-fundraising.org.uk); and Coutts Bank, in association with the Centre for Philanthropy, Humanitarianism and Social Justice at the University of Kent, produces annually 'The Coutts Million Pound Donors Report' (www.coutts.com/files/million-pound-donors-report-2010.pdf).

come in anyway through spontaneous gifts, and, much more important, would have been obtained by academic departments and colleges through personal contacts with persons interested in their field. The latter are particularly important at Oxford and Cambridge and other places with established strength in scientific research.

2. The figures include money raised to pay for current expenditure. Traditionally, university fund-raising, at Oxford and Cambridge at least, was confined to seeking capital endowments and gifts of buildings (and related physical assets). Endowments provide a secure stream of income; gifts of buildings provide benefits in kind (subject to a financial liability for their maintenance and depreciation if that is not adequately provided for). But money raised for current expenditure is different. It is an insecure form of income: if the gifts decline it may not be possible to pay the bills. If it is obtained by employing fund-raisers, the university (or college) becomes dependent on them, and they will tend to gain the bureaucratic power that comes from being and feeling indispensable.

Understandably, it looks as if gifts for current expenditure have been taken to the greatest extent by the new universities that need money but lack high research status and rich alumni.

There is much evidence of American influence:

1. In 2006 a report by the Sutton Trust, an educational charity, noted that:

> ...the rapid expansion of development offices has outstripped the supply of suitably qualified development professionals. It is currently an employees market, with salaries rising significantly and universities having to recruit from the US and Canada. In some universities this has had the unfortunate effect of fuelling further scepticism of the value of fund-raising among academics – many of whom are paid much less than senior development professionals.[10]

2. In 2007 it was reported that eight UK universities employed fund-raisers from the United States or Canada: Oxford, Nottingham, Durham, Bristol, LSE, Edinburgh, Aston and Warwick.[11]

3. In 2010 Oxford hired a former Yale provost 'to apply his expertise in Ivy League rainmaking to its nearly \$2 billion Oxford Thinking campaign'.[12]

---

10 'University Fundraising – An Update', The Sutton Trust, December 2006.
11 Jessica Shepherd, 'The Americans are coming' *Guardian*, 20 February 2007.
12 *Philanthropy Today*, 8 September 2010. See philanthropy.com/blogs/philanthropytoday/.

The chief message that emerges, often implicitly, from the Ross–CASE surveys is that the way to get money is to follow the American example and cultivate the alumni by employing fund-raisers.

The Applicability of the American Approach to Britain

In Britain, those with money have long felt that their status has come from the class into which they were born or into which they have climbed by such steps as buying a country house, buying a title (by contributing to political parties or to charities that enjoy esteem), taking to blood sports and taking to politics. They have felt no reason to give money to the private school or private university that their parents paid to educate them. Oxford and Cambridge colleges were endowed long ago by donors much motivated by religious feelings that are now forgotten.

The United States is different. Status has been and is acquired by gaining money, displaying it and associating with others who have it; and an important way of displaying it has been by giving to one's university, a phenomenon which American university fund-raisers have cultivated energetically, playing one donor against another, and one generation of alumni against another. Moreover, there is a strong tradition of 'legacy preference', meaning giving preference at admission for the children of alumni, with attention to how much has been given by the family. A number of studies have shown that, despite criticism and partial reforms, legacy preference lives on, not least in the Ivy League; and there is evidence that when a university has reduced legacy preference, the donations it receives have declined.[13]

The American fund-raisers now employed in Britain acknowledge that their tradition is different from that in Britain. In a newspaper article in 2007 one was quoted as saying, 'Where we are from, being asked for donations as a student or alumnus is just an accepted part of university culture'. Another said, 'In the US students are encouraged to feel a sense of belonging to their year group or "class". The class of '73 competes with the class of '74 to raise funds for their college… there is an unabashed notion that it is reasonable to expect people to support their organisation.' A third said, 'My expectation has been that I joined a community for life and that includes being asked for money'.

---

13 See William G. Bowen and Derek Bok, *The Shape of the River* (1998), 28 and 286 fn, who found that a non-black candidate's chances of admission to a small sample of universities were 44 per cent for the children of alumni compared with 22 per cent for children of non-alumni. (The figure for blacks, who may enjoy positive discrimination, was 39 per cent); Jerome Karabel, *The Chosen: the Hidden History of Admission and Exclusion at Harvard, Yale and Princeton* (2005); and Richard D. Kahlenberg (ed.), *Affirmative Action for the Rich: Legacy Preferences in College Admissions* (2010).

But when it came to saying how they proposed to modify the American approach to British conditions, their answers were worryingly imprecise: 'I would feel it was entirely inappropriate to approach a UK donor with that kind of persistence... but we need to stop being embarrassed about asking for money in the UK. I would be sad if in a decade's time students here weren't expecting their universities to ask them for donations.' And, a wonderfully euphemistic reply: 'Effective fundraising doesn't necessarily have to involve badgering. It's about helping people to align their generosity with the university'.[14]

From this it would seem that the main strategy of the imported American fund-raisers and their British disciples is to seek tactfully to appeal across the board to the alumni of their university, hoping that they will in time respond like Americans, even if no equivalent of legacy preference is imported. In this they may have a rather greater chance of success in Britain than on the Continent, since the Americanisation of society and its values has gone further here.

Fund-Raising at Cambridge

In October 1987 a University Development Office was set up under a full-time fund-raiser, and in November 1988 the Cambridge Foundation, an equivalent of the old Cambridge University Association, was created to appeal for money.[15] In keeping with the times, the composition of its board, some selected from the academic community in Cambridge, others from the corporate world, the arts, and politics is strikingly different from that of the patrician body of titled persons that ran the CUA, as can be seen from a comparison of Table 8.6 below with Table 4.4.

The Cambridge colleges severally have also created development offices, with the result that there has been a remarkable growth in the number of persons employed in fund-raising at Cambridge. In 2010 the total was 142, about half working for the colleges, half for the university. Of the university's staff, 18 were employed at the office on Madison Avenue of 'Cambridge in America', the Development Office's New York outpost.

At Cambridge – I do not know the practice at other places – the cost of fund-raising is paid by the university and colleges. The latest figure for the university's costs is £6.8 million in 2009–2010. Of this, nearly £3 million

---

14 Jessica Shepherd, 'The Americans are coming', *Guardian*, 20 February 2007.
15 'Report of the Council of the Senate on the establishment of a University Development Unit', *Cambridge University Reporter*, 18 February 1987, 354–5; and 'Cambridge Foundation: Notice', *Cambridge University Reporter*, 20 June 1990, 867–8.

Table 8.7. The patrons and trustees of the Cambridge Foundation in 2010

Patron
HRH the Duke of Edinburgh, Chancellor of the University

Vice-Patrons
Mr Peter Beckwith (property)
Lady Judge (law and business)

Trustees
The Lord Watson of Richmond, Chairman, (journalism, business and politics)
Professor Dame Alison Richard, Vice-Chairman, Vice-Chancellor of the University

Mr Nicholas Baring (banking)
The Right Hon. Lord Browne of Madingley (petroleum)
Sir Geoffrey Cass (publishing)
Mr Douglas Daft (soft drinks)
Dr William H. Janeway (fund management)

Professor Jane Heal
Professor Jeremy Saunders
Professor Dame Jean Thomas
Sir David Wallace

Trustees Emeritus
Sir Paul Judge (food)
Sir David K P Li (banking)
Sir Martin Sorrell (advertising)

Table 8.8. The number of fund-raisers employed at Cambridge

	1999	2008	2010
Colleges	34	62	68
University Development Office	23	67	74
Total	57	129	142

Source: The figures for 2008 and 2010, supplied the Development Office, are for full-time equivalent staff. The 1999 figures were estimated by applying to the 2008 figure the proportionate change between 1999 and 2008 in the number of entries in the university telephone book with respect to colleges and the Development Office under the headings development director, alumni office etc.

went on staff costs, nearly £4 million on 'other operating costs', meaning expenditure on publicity, events, travel, alumni magazines, rent and so on.[16] In the same year the colleges spent £7.1 million: the combined total was just under £14 million.

---

16 *Cambridge University Reporter*, Special no. 9, 18 January 2011, 20.

The 800th Anniversary Appeal

After the University Development Office had been in operation for nearly two decades, the university announced on 22 September 2005 that, together with the colleges, it was 'launching a major global fundraising campaign today, aiming to raise £1 billion by 2012' to celebrate the 800th anniversary of the foundation of the university.[17] In the campaign report for 2009–2010 it was announced that a total of £1.037 billion had been raised. The words used in the statement of financial performance in that report were these: 'As a result of this year's success the former vice-chancellor, Professor Dame Alison Richard was able to announce in June 2010 that the campaign had passed the £1 billion milestone, two years ahead of the date anticipated at the public launch in 2005.'[18] The raising of more than a billion in five years seems a remarkable achievement. But, as can be seen from Table 8.3, that is not what was achieved. A large part (39 per cent) of the money was raised in the five years before the campaign was launched in 2005.

It seems that when the decision was made to conduct a campaign, the announcement of a target was put off for a few years in order to allow time to judge the rate at which money might come in. There need be objection to that way of doing things; apparently it is standard practice in the profession.[19] What

Table 8.9. The composition of the billion pounds, including pledges, raised by the 800th anniversary appeal

	Raised in 2001–2005	Raised in 2006–2010	Total	Increase from 2001–5 to 2006–10
	£ million			£ million / %
University	238.8	338.6	577.4	99.8 (42 %)
Colleges	162.8	297.3	460.1	134.5 (83 %)
Total	401.6	635.9	1,037.5	234.3 (58 %)

17 University of Cambridge press release, 22 September 2005.

18 'The Cambridge 800th Anniversary Campaign Report 2009–2010' (University of Cambridge, n.d.), 6. Similar words were used were used on other pages by the co-chairmen of the campaign and the vice-chancellor. The chairman of the College's Committee, Professor Martin Daunton, referred to the start of the campaign 'in 2001–2002'.

19 The 2009–10 Ross–CASE survey reported that 36 universities were conducting a 'capital campaign' (like the 800th anniversary appeal at Cambridge) and says: 'The public phases of these campaigns were expected to last a mean of just over three and a half years. The mean proportion of the capital campaign target the universities expected to achieve before the campaign was launched was 41 per cent, with a median of 40 per cent.' I think this means that, typically, a target figure was chosen of which 40 per cent was already in hand, a figure close to Cambridge's 39 per cent.

is surprising is the manner in which the results of the Cambridge campaign were announced. What was said was strictly speaking true, but it was likely to cause the innocent reader to conclude that the £1 billion was raised in half the time it in fact took. It is unclear whether the university will gain or lose from the probable misconception by many of the success of the campaign. It may be hoped that potential donors, rather than hold back in the belief that essential needs must have been met, will feel they must join in an apparently swelling herd of donors. When in 2010 Oxford produced similar results, it made plain how long it had taken to raise its money.[20]

The money raised by the university during the 800th anniversary campaign and adjacent years has one conspicuous component that has implications both for accounting and for fund-raising policy: big gifts that would, certainly or probably, have been given anyway.

During the years 2001–2010 three really big gifts came to the university: $210 million from the Bill and Melinda Gates Foundation to finance Gates Cambridge scholarships; £49.7 million from Dr Herchel Smith to endow a number of new chairs and some research fellowships; and £82 million from Lord Sainsbury's Gatsby Foundation to build the Sainsbury Laboratory for the study of plant sciences.[21] All three look as if they were given regardless of the 800th anniversary campaign. Yet the last two were included in the £1.037 billion that the campaign announced it had raised by 2010, while the first, the Gates gift, was excluded, as were the sums raised by the Commonwealth and related trusts.[22] One can see two possible grounds for these exclusions: the decisions to make these gifts predated, in part or whole, 2001, the beginning of the campaign's accounting period; and those responsible for the gifts, the Gates family and Dr Seal, might have objected to the suggestion that they were led by the fund-raisers.

The policy problem is this. Gifts that are solicited by members of departments and faculties who reach out to, or are approached by, rich persons connected with their subject have a tiny cost per pound raised, compared with gifts (including bequests), mostly small, that are obtained by employing fund-raisers to cultivate alumni with dinners, parties, magazines,

20   *Oxford Thinking, And Doing: Where the Money's Going, Where the Thinking's Going – A Report on the Campaign for the University of Oxford at 31 January 2010*, www.ox.ac.uk/document. rm?id=1598 (accessed 27 February 2012).

21   For details of Dr Herchel Smith's bequest see 'Notice of Bequest', *Cambridge University Reporter*, 19 June 2002; for details of the Gatsby foundation founded in 1967 by David Sainsbury (now Lord Sainsbury and vice-chancellor of the university), see www.gatsby. org.uk.

22   Development Office report 'New funds Raised B', *Campaign Reports Graphs 20101103*, acknowledges the problem by giving figures excluding as well as figures including the Gates and Herchel Smith bequests.

entertainments, telephone calls and the like. To decide which of these two lines, or what combination of them, to pursue, their costs and benefits need to be analysed and compared by persons other than the fund-raisers, who are interested parties. It is not clear how far that has been done by the university or the colleges. Moreover, consideration needs to be given to the implications of introducing a rising population of fund-raisers, whose task is persuasion, into communities of academics whose task is to seek and teach the truth.

The Fruits of the 800th Anniversary Appeal

The £577 million recorded as the university's gain from the 800th appeal was made up as follows:

	£ million
Buildings	222
Endowment	199
Current use	156
Total	577

The increase in endowment capital rises to about £350 million if we include the gifts from the Gates Foundation and the Commonwealth and related trusts.

The extent to which the endowment income of the university has been increased by this accretion of funds can be put at approximately £13 million a year. In addition, some of the money given for current use will have been earning interest, so that the total addition to endowment income including interest may be nearer to £15 million.[23] That, in combination with the university's investment performance (measured on the new total return basis), has been enough to make endowment income (including interest) keep up with the growth of other types of income in this period of expansion, but endowment income still accounts for only 6 per cent of the university's total income and is forecast to stay at that level (Table 8.2).

The endowment income of the colleges is now about 50 per cent greater than that of the university: £72 million compared with £48 million.[24] Of that £78 million, £28 million is the endowment income of Trinity. Taking a long view, the university has done a lot of catching up since 1850, when its endowment

---

23 Estimate made with the assistance of Mr Paul Light using figures from the university's accounts and the Development Office report 'New funds Raised B', *Campaign Reports Graphs*.

24 See Appendix 8A.

Table 8.10. The composition of 'other income' in 2009

	£ million
Services rendered	26.4
Health/hospital authorities	16.0
Conferences etc	7.5
University companies	18.0
Transfer from Cambridge Assessment (exams)	14.9
Rental income	6.5
Unrestricted donations	12.1
Released from capital grants	8.7
Sundry income	17.6
Total	127.7

Source: *Cambridge University Reporter*, Special no. 9, 18 January 2011, Financial Management Information for the year ending 31 July 2010, 5.

income was one-twentieth of that of the colleges. This has been principally because gifts have been so heavily concentrated on the physical sciences which, since the mid-nineteenth century, have been based in the university, not the colleges. Before then there were some small college laboratories.

Other Income

This residual category contains a ragbag of items, including income from charges for the use of university facilities by outsiders, and a transfer of £14.9 million from the examination syndicate, now re-christened 'Cambridge Assessment'. This is one of the payments that are extracted from time to time from the examination syndicate and the university press, those large wholly owned subsidiaries of the university that seem to have been rather adept at resisting surrender of their profits to their owner.

The Budgetary Forecast

The report on the financial position of the university and the budget for 2011–12, published in May 2011, forecasts that in 2014–15 total income and expenditure will be about 9 per cent lower in real terms than in 2009–10. The main changes assumed are a 21 per cent cut in the government grant and a 62 per cent increase in fees; endowment income is assumed to increase by 6 per cent; inflation is assumed to continue.[25]

---

25 *Cambridge University Reporter*, 25 May 2011, 5 and 12–13.

Table 8.11. The pattern of expenditure in 2009

Percentages	
Direct costs	
Arts humanities and social sciences	11
Physical and biological sciences, technology, and medicine	53
Other academic depts. and	2
Subtotal	*66*
Overheads	
Libraries computing etc.	5
Estate management and building services	10
Administration	7
Staff and student services	1
Other	10
Subtotal	*34*
Total	100

Source: *Cambridge University Reporter*, Financial Management Information for the year ending 31 July 2009, Special no. 9, 12 January 2010, section C, 17–21.

Expenditure

For the most part the evolution of expenditure matches the evolution of income that we have examined and merits no new comment (Table 8.11). Two features stand out:

1. Expenditure on the physical sciences is now nearly five times that on the arts and humanities. This is because the buildings, apparatus and other inputs required for research and teaching of the physical sciences have become so costly. In number, the ratio of science to arts students has increased only a little, more in the case of undergraduates than postgraduates (Appendix 8A).
2. Just over one-third of spending goes on overheads. High expenditure on buildings and computing, which together account for 19 per cent of total spending, is understandable: new laboratories and other buildings are expensive, and so are computer facilities. It is the figure for central administration, including the Development Office – 6 per cent of the total, or £50 million – that makes one raise one's eyebrows. This growth of the bureaucracy merits further examination.

The Growth of Bureaucracy

The nature of jobs and the categorisation of them in university offices have changed so much since the 1939–45 war that it has not been possible to

Table 8.12. The growth of administrative expenditure, 1986 to 2009

	1986	2000	2009
A. Indices of expenditure deflated by HEFCE index			
Administration, incl. Development Office	100	300	527
Total expenditure	100	213	292
B. Money value of expenditure – £ million			
Administration	3.4	17.0	44.0
Development Office	Neg.	2.2	5.6
Total expenditure	90.0	360.0	728.0
Admin. and Dev. Office as % of total expenditure	*3.8*	*5.3*	*6.8*

Source: *Cambridge University Reporter*, Special no. 11, 20 February 1987, 8; Special no. 8, 20 December 2000, 16; and Special no. 9, 12 January 2010, 14, 20 and 28.

measure satisfactorily the growth of bureaucracy since then. What one knows is that after the war the bureaucracy was still very small and manned at the top by academics. That is not the case now. For the past two decades there are reliable data on expenditure and on numbers employed in administration that permit us to see what has happened.

University expenditure under the heading administration, deflated by the index of university costs, has increased fivefold since 1986, while total university income has increased threefold. The share of expenditure going to administration, including the Development Office, has risen from 3.8 to 6.8 per cent of total expenditure.

As to numbers, we have figures for 'Officers in institutions placed under the supervision of the Council', a category that excludes, for example, custodians and maintenance staff, and also excludes the office of the vice-chancellor, including its press office and similar new appendages. The numbers, which may not perfectly match the expenditure category 'Administration' in Table 9.2, more than doubled between 2000 and 2009 (Table 9.3). The number in finance, management services and what is now called human resources was in each case approximately tripled; the number in academic affairs, research services and estate management rose less rapidly. The number of students and the number of academic staff in the university both increased by only 4 per cent.[26]

I have not attempted to analyse in detail the steps by which this extraordinary expansion in the bureaucracy of the university came about.

---

26 Student numbers, from *Cambridge University Reporter*, Special no. 4, 8 October 2009, 4, were 16,699 in 2000 and 17,398 in 2009; the number of academic staff, established and unestablished, was 1,529 in 2000 and 1,593 in 2009.

Table 8.13. The number of 'officers' in university offices, 2000 and 2009

	2000		2009	Multiple
Estate management	40		56	1.4
Finance	17		51	3.0
General board + registry	56	Academic + secretariat	100	1.8
Management inf. services	18		51	3.1
Personnel	10	Human resources	33	2.8
Research services	8		8	1.0
External affairs and communications			10	
Total	149		309	2.1

Source: 'Officers in institutions placed under the supervision of the council' from *Cambridge University Reporter*, Special no. 3, 2000 and Special no. 7, 2009.

One can see some explanations. The administrative regime inherited in 1945 relied on the willingness of some dons to give some of their time to administration and a few to take to it full time. It was rather insular and conservative, yet it could be flexible: in the inter-war and post-war years many new courses were introduced, and research in physics and other sciences flourished brilliantly. Relations with the government in the shape of the UGC were then informal, the independence of the universities was respected, and government regulation of society was generally minimal. Faculties and departments did not suffer much time-consuming attention from the central administration.

One can see several intertwined causes of the growth of bureaucracy since then:

1. Even if there had been no increase in government regulation, an increase in the number of administrative staff, including experts in, for example, computers and in the safeguarding and exploitation of intellectual property, would have been needed to manage the increase in the income of the university from increasingly diverse sources and the increase in the diversity of specialised subjects of research and teaching on which that income is spent.

2. There has been a torrent of government regulations, coming partly from Brussels, that apply to the whole economy, for example, rules concerning planning, health and safety, human rights, labour law, freedom of information and visas.

3. Since the re-labelling of polytechnics as universities and the replacement of the UGC by HEFCE, there has been an increasing flow of regulations applied to universities along with other institutions of higher education.

4. The pressure on academics to produce research articles must have discouraged them from engaging in part-time administrative work, which they used to perform with informal efficiency since they knew the academic world and its inhabitants. In their place, there appears to have been a tendency to appoint persons trained in management techniques that require analytical staff and copious statistics for their application.

Clearly a larger and in some cases more professional bureaucracy was needed. But one must question whether it had to be so large. When a bureaucratic regime is reshaped, there is always a danger that the new men and new women who design it will, in the name of efficiency, divide tasks and recruit staff on a grander scale than is necessary. As Professor Parkinson observed years ago after studying the growth of the British civil service, the expanded staff will not be idle, they will make work for one another. They will be busy demanding information from those they manage and from their colleagues, and hurrying from meeting to meeting.[27]

---

27 C. Northcote Parkinson, *Parkinson's Law or the Pursuit of Progress* (1958), and with respect to the American universities, see Benjamin Ginsberg, *The Fall of the Faculty: The Rise of the All-Administrative University and Why It Matters* (2011).

Appendix 8A: Income of the Colleges and the University, 1946 to 2012 Forecast

	1946	1966	1986	2009	2012 forecast
	£ thousand			£ million	
Colleges					
Endowment income, incl. trusts	525	1,751	20.0	72.4*	
University					
Endowment income, incl. trusts	275	846	4.9	47.7	50
Fees	89	625	12.2	91.8	118
Contribution from colleges	54	169	0	0	0
Non-government research grants etc.	5	403	7.2	147.7	183
Other	20	50	5.7	132.4	126
Government general grants	257	6,619	45.6	205.2	194
Government research grants/contracts	149	561	13.2	112.5	130
Subtotal – government	406	7,180	58.8	317.7	331
Total university income	849	9,273	88.8	737.3	801
Index of university costs	*100*	*270*	*1,980*	*5,421*	
Total income deflated by costs	*100*	*384*	*531*	*1,622*	
Student numbers					2009/ 1946
a. Undergraduates	5,765	8,168	9,720	11,816	× 2.0
b. Postgraduates	909	1,775	2,844	5,582	× 6.1
Total	6,674	9,943	12,564	17,398	× 2.6
Arts:science ratio					
a. Undergraduates	58:42	52:48	50:50	45:55	
b. Postgraduates	51:49	51:49	49:51	47:53	
Total	56:44	52:48	50:50	47:53	

* 2008, after which the method of calculating college income was changed.
Sources: University income from *Cambridge University Reporter*, 13 January 1947; 15 December 1966; Special no. 11, 1986–87; Special no. 9, 2009–10. College income for 1945–46 from 'Report of the Financial Board, 23 April 1947', CUA Min. II; later years from entries for 'College contributions in the financial year…' in the *Cambridge University Reporter*. Student numbers for 1946 and 1966 from 'Report of the General Board on the long term development of the University, 4 December 1974', *Cambridge University Reporter*, 17 December 1974, 546, 570 and 572; 1986 and 2009 from *Cambridge University Reporter*, Special no. 4, 8 October 2009, 4.

Appendix 8B: Research Grants Received by Different Subjects 2009

Research grants received by different subjects 2009

	£ million	% of total
Arts, humanities and social sciences	20.2	8
Physical sciences	62.2	24
Technology, incl. engineering	39.0	15
Biological sciences*	66.6	26
Clinical medicine	68.9	27
Other	2.7	1
Total	259.6	100

* Of which, plant sciences 3.7, veterinary medicine 4.0

Source: *Cambridge University Reporter*, Special no. 9, Financial Management Information for the year ending 31 July 2009, 22–7.

INDEX

The letter *t* following a page number denotes a table.

Printed in the USA
CPSIA information can be obtained
at www.ICGtesting.com
JSHW082148140824
68134JS00002B/41

9 780857 285157